B-SIDE BOOKS

PUBLIC BOOKS SERIES

PUBLIC BOOKS SERIES

Sharon Marcus and Caitlin Zaloom, Editors

Founded in 2012, *Public Books* is required reading for anyone interested
in what scholars have to say about contemporary culture, politics, and
society. The monographs, anthologies, surveys, and experimental formats
featured in this series translate the online experience of intellectual
creativity and community into the physical world of print. Through
writing that exemplifies the magazine's commitment to expertise,
accessibility, and diversity, the Public Books Series aims to break
down barriers between the academy and the public in order
to make the life of the mind a public good.

■ ■ ■

Think in Public: A Public Books Reader, edited by Sharon Marcus and Caitlin
Zaloom, 2019
Antidemocracy in America: Truth, Power, and the Republic at Risk, edited by Eric
Klinenberg, Caitlin Zaloom, and Sharon Marcus, 2019

B-SIDE BOOKS

Essays on Forgotten Favorites

EDITED BY

JOHN PLOTZ

Columbia University Press

New York

Columbia University Press
Publishers Since 1893
New York   Chichester, West Sussex
cup.columbia.edu
Copyright © 2021 Columbia University Press
All rights reserved

Library of Congress Cataloging-in-Publication Data
Names: Plotz, John, 1967– editor.
Title: B-side books : essays on forgotten favorites /
edited by John Plotz.
Description: New York : Columbia University Press, [2021] |
Series: Public books series | Includes bibliographical references.
Identifiers: LCCN 2020053471 (print) | LCCN 2020053472 (ebook) |
ISBN 9780231200561 (hardback ; acid-free paper) |
ISBN 9780231200578 (trade paperback ; acid-free paper) |
ISBN 9780231553681 (ebook)
Subjects: LCSH: Canon (Literature) | Best books. | Criticism.
Classification: LCC PN81 .B24 2021 (print) | LCC PN81 (ebook) |
DDC 809—dc23
LC record available at https://lccn.loc.gov/2020053471
LC ebook record available at https://lccn.loc.gov/2020053472

Printed in the United States of America

Cover design: Julia Kushnirsky
Cover photograph: AGIP—Rue des Archives / Granger, NYC

To David,
through thick and thin, without fail and without doubt

Writing means being overheard.
—Zadie Smith, *Intimations*

CONTENTS

CONTENTS

CONTENTS

CONTENTS

CONTENTS

FOREWORD

SHARON MARCUS

B-SIDE BOOKS is a book of books. It features writers writing about rare, forgotten, and unsung works that changed their lives and could change yours.

A guide for anyone who has ever found themselves perplexed about what to select in a library or bookstore, *B-Side Books* is an atlas for novice explorers, picky readers, contrarians drawn to what other people *aren't* reading, and epicures who seek to go beyond this year's most notable books.

The essays collected here proffer delightfully unusual suggestions about *what* to read. More importantly, they also model *how* to read. In the spirit of *Public Books*, B-Side Books provides the distinctive savor and savvy that come from blending expertise with pleasure, rigor with enthusiasm, and scholarship with appreciation.

Caitlin Zaloom and I launched *Public Books* in 2012 as an online magazine designed to bring specialized knowledge to a general public. Initially, we focused on covering newly released works. After a few years, we sought a way to highlight great books of older vintage, books with tiny or nonexistent reputations that deserved more attention. In keeping with our magazine's title, which celebrates analog print culture in the digital era, we called these essays "B-Sides," after the obscure tracks that used to appear on the opposite sides of hit singles released as 45-rpm records.

Under the expert guidance of series editor John Plotz, "B-Sides" became a paean to unsung, underrecognized genius. I teach literature for a living and make a point of seeking out obscure writers, yet I had heard of few and read almost none of these minor masterpieces until encountering them in these essays.

■ ■ ■

B-Side books are not always easy to love at first sight. Unlike classics, they do not come to us enveloped in the glamor of the *déjà lu*, the always-already-read books that have for decades been taught, adapted, and turned into cultural touchstones. It is easier to appreciate *Jane Eyre* knowing—as most readers today do—that a "madwoman in the attic" haunts its pages or to tackle *Ulysses* informed that it updates an ancient Greek epic or to approach *The Bluest Eye* cognizant that its title evokes racist beauty standards. Understanding paves the way for enjoyment.

But whereas classics come to us cooked, B-Side books come to us raw. The essays in this collection prepare unfamiliar works for consumption by marshalling the knowledge and devotion that allows for a new kind of appreciation. These essays combine, in perfect proportions, the obsessiveness of the scholar, the discernment of the critic, and the effusiveness of the fan. And in so doing, they demonstrate some of the best ways to read.

First, the contributors to this volume, by deploying their formidable knowledge, make unfamiliar works less strange by placing them in context. Some of our essayists situate their chosen texts historically, as when Lauren Kaminsky and Steven Biel help us understand what makes *The Forbidden Zone* an even more brilliant representation of modern warfare than better-known books about World War I by Erich Marie Remarque and Ernest Hemingway. Stephanie Burt draws on her impressive grasp of all kinds of poetry to help us hear what Patience Agbabi has in common with both the Victorian poet Algernon Swinburne and present-day rap artists. Other contributors link little-known works to well-known genres, such as dystopian sci-fi, the fable, the coming-of-age story, and Central European political novels about disillusionment (are there any other kind?). Still others show how minor masterpieces generate their own categories: "nice art" (Andrew Miller on Joe Brainard); the revisionist anti-western (John Plotz on John Williams); middle-class vacations gone bad (Margaret Cohen on Erskine Childress); the literature of parental insomnia (Leah Price on Celia Fremlin); and espionage novels that equate spies with ghosts (Penny Fielding on Graham Greene).

Next, by attending to craft, these essays teach us to identify and revel in the grain of an author's voice, the lilt of their sentences, the glint of their observations. Stephen McCauley, a fiction writer and teacher of creative writing, shows how Christopher Isherwood compresses a wealth of information about not one but two characters into the brief dialogue tag "growled crossly." Emily Hyde shows how "parataxis"—the practice of piling up words and phrases with no coordination—perfectly expresses the "jumpy, unhinged" rhythm of postcolonial life in Dennis Williams's *Other Leopards*. Carlo Rotella identifies how Charles Portis's *Gringos* mixes "dire grandiosity" with "easygoing self-deprecation," showing us how to understand *and* enjoy this little-read novel.

Finally, as enthusiastic fans, this volume's authors attend to their own reading experiences. They tell us how they discovered books that delighted them, provoked them, and changed them and how their love for these books has evolved since those first encounters. Kathryn Lofton offers a wry but moving assessment of her early reading of Edith Hamilton's *Mythology*, which set her on a path to becoming a queer scholar of religion. Adrienne Brown writes of encountering underrepresented experiences of modernity in Paule Marshall's *Brown Girl, Brownstones*. Love makes these writers better critics, set on distilling what their favorite texts can teach us. Sylvia Townsend Warner's *Lolly Willowes* shows us that domesticity can be wild and revolutionary; Dambudzo Marechera's *The House of Hunger*, "how certain lives get designated as disposable"; William Hope Hodgson's *The House on the Borderland*, "just how uneasily we sit within the endless spinning of time."

■ ■ ■

The contributors to *B-Side Books* help us love what they love by sharing their knowledge and their passion. The catchphrase "everyone's a critic" usually evokes how depressingly easy it is to be a killjoy, to find reasons not to like things, to make anything look bad. The contributors to this volume give this old saying a magical new spin: they make everyone a critic capable of seeing what is great and lovely and instructive in obscure books that might otherwise have eluded our grasp.

ACKNOWLEDGMENTS

PUBLIC BOOKS supplied this volume's name and so much more. For the original inspiration and plenty of room to run with it, hearty thanks to Sharon Marcus and Caitlin Zaloom. Liz Maynes-Amizade played a vital early role; Stephen Twiley and later Ben Platt were steadfast and generous editors, buttressed by superbly scrupulous copyeditors: Tristan Beach, Lou Ellingson, Caitlin Fleming, Annie Galvin, Leslie Kriesel, Bernadette Malvarca, Kirsten O'Regan, and Mimi Vu. Matthew Schratz, then hard at work completing his PhD at Brandeis, was a great research assistant; Lisa Pannella and Leah Steele were of huge indirect assistance. At Columbia University Press, Philip Leventhal and such hard-working team members as Monique Briones were generous and indispensable.

My truest thanks go to all the B-side authors who dug deep into their pasts and gave of their time in the present. I know that they share my gratitude to *Public Books* and Columbia

University Press; I also know that each of them has debts of gratitude to friends and family akin to the ones spelled out below. So imagine a forty-fold multiplication of what follows.

As always, love and gratitude to the heart-fast friends who have suggested books or authors or simply talked through the every question that matters—and some that don't: Liberty Aldrich, George Boulukos, Amanda Claybaugh, Theo Davis, Elizabeth Ferry, Robert Glick, Daniel Itzkovitz, Phil Joseph, Ivan Kreilkamp, Yoon Sun Lee, Chaela Pastore, Leah Price, Martin Puchner, Linda Schlossberg, Eugene Sheppard, Gillian Silverman, Vanessa Smith, Alex Star, Lucy Vinten, Rachel Yassky.

Family often but should not go without saying. Everything I can imagine accomplishing, and everything that makes it worth bothering, comes from their love, support and inspiration. My parents, Paul and Judith Plotz; the inimitable Lisa Soltani (the family you choose is best of all); and the indispensable if soon-departing Alan and Daria: without you I'm nothing. Finally, this book is dedicated to my one and only brother, the handsomest, baldest, tallest panda-hater I know. Whenever I read about the fraternal bond of union solidarity, or the French pledge of *Liberté, Egalité, Fraternité*, you come straight to mind.

INTRODUCTION

JOHN PLOTZ

B-SIDE BOOKS recaptures the moment when someone leans across a dinner table or an aisle or any of those spaces that exist to be crossed to tell you about a book. Some leaners use the word *love*; others just want to convey the thrill of discovering a writer for the first time. There may be facts and figures or a few lines imperfectly quoted. Often it is their tone rather than the words: *this matters*. And every so often a detail they cite will strike you so deeply that, thinking back on the book years later, it is that moment you remember. A B-Side moment.

Some of these pieces recount sudden epiphanies; others recount a slow burn, admiration forged over years or decades or sanctified by rereading. Beneath all that cogitation lurks affection, affiliation, and well concealed passion. My editorial role—recruiting authors, whittling down a dream list, helping them redraft so that their pieces both revealed what they knew and conveyed what they felt—amounted to unlocking a barn door and standing back while the horses bolted out to pasture. These are essays about getting drawn in, and about why it could happen to you, too. Looking back, it makes perfect sense that my own B-Side was about sudden death by water. When books have a real hold on you, a seemingly placid flow suddenly turns furious. Nothing in what follows is as peaceful as it seems.

Some writers (Zorach, Saint-Amour, Lofton) begin with a book read in childhood then returned to in maturity. But that overt gap between childish and mature reading is only the outward and visible sign of a more general process every B-Side writer undergoes. All of these pieces rediscover an earlier feeling (*what a book!*) and get to work turning that reading into writing. You might even say they try to write reading.

The idea of loving your subject matter may raise eyebrows in some circles: do biologists love fruit flies? (Based on my own summer lab job, I'm going to say, yes, sometimes they do.) This book invites that kind of overinvestment. Every letter to a prospective contributor started with the request to think of "a book unjustly kicked to history's curb, either an outlier from a great writer or an unexpected gem from somebody thoroughly forgotten." Then it urged writers to think about how their own love might be turned into something transmissible to others.

In her preface, Sharon Marcus highlights the significance of naming these pieces after the obscure songs on the flipside of old records. These books are forgotten cousins to the canon, and they elicit proprietary passion. What these writers have unearthed made them want to stop, to ponder, to draw out their discovery in enough detail that you could see it as well.

Looking back over the B-Sides I have edited for *Public Books*, I was struck by how many aim to reveal not so much a completed thought as the process of thinking. My daughter Daria once pointed out that on the storytelling show *The Moth*, stories almost always pivot on the phrase: "in that moment, I realized." B-Sides too often unfold around just such situational realizations. Ursula K. Le Guin senses John Galt writing against violence by writing a nonviolent world into being. Vanessa Smith feels readerly attunement with Marion Milner's joy in the unconscious expertise of ping-pong, when the player's hand seems to move toward the ball of its own accord.

The pieces are grouped in sections to suit readerly moods: on days when you have a yen to fantasize, you might turn to "Other Worlds"—on another day, nostalgia might send you toward "Home Fires." However, there are as many ways in as there are readers—you might even pick a name on impulse. Or tumble the book over and let fate choose.

Treat *B-Side Books* as an atlas that redirects readerly traffic from broad avenues to winding byways. In that guise, it defies easy summary. In one sense these pieces are profoundly connected by the passion that runs through them. But in another sense that is what divides them. Because these writers were urged to embrace an idiosyncratic attachment, no two objects are alike. Theo Davis cottons on to a Japanese Buddhist nun's search for enlightenment while Maud Ellman loves *Lady Into Fox* (the title says it all). Meanwhile, Toril Moi takes late-night

London rambles with Helen De Witt's *The Last Samurai* and Margaret Cohen thinks about the operation of actual sand in *The Riddle of the Sands*. These are pieces pursued with what Theodor Adorno called *Sabbath-day contemplation*—the sort of attention you go on giving even when the working week has ended.

These B-Sides embody the companionship we find in words and ideas beyond the classroom and library and book group. Every book is its own desert island: we read, as we live, alone. Yet inside the cocoon created by the favorite chair or the nighttime ritual, readers want both privacy *and* communion. Solitude sometimes loves company. May you find it here.

PART I

CHILDHOOD, THROUGH A GLASS DARKLY

TO SOME writers, the childishness of childhood retains its power of soothing simplicity. Toril Moi is thrilled by Helen DeWitt's capacious praise of the boy prodigy Ludo's quest for an (ever-receding, possibly imaginary) father figure. Elizabeth Ferry finds in the juvenile *Diary of Helen Morley* (translated by Elizabeth Bishop) a book that "day by day, minute by minute . . . keeps that sense of real happening alive" and "breathes actuality." A similarly delighted sense of that lost world in all its manifold absurdity pervades Caleb Crain's celebration of the "silly satire" *The Young Visiters*, written by the nine-year-old (yes, you read that right) Daisy Ashford. That novel features this sublime sentence: "I am not quite a gentleman . . . but you would hardly notice it but cant be helped anyhow."

Though childhood may have such moments of sweetness, some authors glimpse desolation beneath. Adrienne Brown manages to find radiance in "the intricacies of Black becoming within a largely Black world," but *Brown Girl, Brownstones* also gives a view from below of "crisscrossed and ever-moving lines—lines of color but also class, gender, nationality, sexuality and age" that make up midcentury Brooklyn. Similarly, there is much more than just "pluck and the swamp" in Gene Stratton-Porter's *A Girl of the Limberlost* (1909). Rebecca Zorach unfolds the ways in which the maternal desire for stasis, even as it seems to throttle the heroine's ambitions, simultaneously incarnates a powerful ecological impulse in favor of "wild nature." The novelist Salvatore Scibona felt "my mind bec[oming] the page," during a youthful first encounter with *An American Childhood*, Annie Dillard's poetic memoir of a Pittsburgh childhood. Looking back over the decades, he grasps the anguish interwoven with the book's beautifully neutral observational style and concludes that "we grow egos in order to save ourselves from upheavals like this."

Chapter One

A GIRL OF THE LIMBERLOST

GENE STRATTON-PORTER

REBECCA ZORACH

ALL BUT forgotten today, Gene Stratton-Porter was—in the early twentieth century—an immensely popular novelist, essayist, naturalist, photographer, and film producer. Damning her with faint praise, the Yale critic William Lyon Phelps took her (with Zane Grey and Harold Bell Wright) as the basis for an essay called "The Virtues of the Second Rate." Her best-known novel, *A Girl of the Limberlost* (1909), initially may well seem a sentimental coming-of-age story. Yet the author's commitment to ecological preservation, woven through her midwestern romance plot, gives the novel a continuing resonance that is quirky and unexpected.

Far more than just a sequel to Stratton-Porter's *Freckles* (1904), *A Girl of the Limberlost* tells the story of a second-generation settler girl growing up near the Limberlost Swamp, a vast northeastern Indiana wetland that was at that moment being busily drained for timber, farming, and oil drilling.

Elnora Comstock is a diamond in the rough, a country girl trying to make good by attending high school in the nearby "city"
(actually a small town). Stratton-Porter captures the burning
shame of poverty and awkwardness but doesn't let Elnora lin-
ger long in it. She has pluck and friends to help her and most of
all she has the swamp itself. The natural world provides not
only comfort but also (unexpected plot twist!) economic subsis-
tence in the form of the moths she sells to collectors.

As a coming-of-age story *Girl of the Limberlost* can be a little
too blunt in its didacticism. But prescient ecological consciousness ensures that its pleasures aren't all spun sugar and sunlight.
Butterflies feast on carrion; birds may be photographed; but
moths are *collected*. When the Bird Woman uses the word,
Elnora replies, "That 'collected' frightens me. I've only gath-
ered." But making a collection to instruct the world about the
beauties of nature requires a killing jar. The other things Elnora
gathers and sells are artifacts: "stone axes, arrow points, and
Indian pipes." The book (like the very name Indiana) is haunted
by the Indigenous people driven off their land in the preceding
century. In the world of the Limberlost, the gloom and danger
of the swamp—named, after all, for a man whose life was lost
there—and the sumptuousness of its beauties intermingle just
as human violence and human goodness do.

One reason the book has stuck with me from childhood is
that the place of nature's bounty in Elnora's story poses some
ethical dilemmas that are subtler than they first appear. The
novel is shaped by tension between a melodramatic plot of
advancement (by way of education, romance, and the door
they open to conventional bourgeois adulthood) and a more

conflicted impulse toward stasis, the maternal desire to freeze things as they are. The palpable tension within such stasis—between an impulse toward preservation and the penumbra of death that necessarily accompanies it—is cast into stark relief by the impeding presence of Elnora's mother, Kate Comstock. Kate lives in a past of her own making, refusing to give her love fully to her daughter because she holds her responsible for the death of her husband.

At the same time, Kate is being urged to sell her property for timber and oil, and she refuses. The swamp is being cleared all around them, but Mrs. Comstock holds firm. It's not because she wants to preserve wild nature. Rather, her preservationist impulse arises from her unwavering and wrongheaded devotion to the memory of a husband who died in the swamp.

Somewhere in Kate's refusal, though, is a kind of restraint that wins a surprising amount of sympathy from the kindly neighbor Margaret Sinton, a surrogate parental figure for Elnora. As Margaret puts it: "S'pose we'd got Elnora when she was a baby, and we'd heaped on her all the love we can't on our own, and we'd coddled, petted, and shielded her, would she have made the woman that living alone, learning to think for herself, and taking all the knocks Kate Comstock could give, have made of her?" Her husband, Wesley, objects that "you can't hurt a child loving it" and Elnora didn't have to suffer "like a poor homeless dog."

Margaret counters that Elnora has a naturally good character but wonders "as we would have raised her, would her heart ever have known the world as it does now? . . . Living life from the rough side has only broadened her." Writ large, Margaret's suggestion is that the right approach to living beings, human or not, might not just be a matter of the proper tending and cultivation of the natural world. Cultivation—as coddling, petting, and shielding—is not the same as care.

The limit case for this overdone cultivation is Chicago, home of Elnora's love interest, Philip Ammon. Chicago figures as a place of spoilage irredeemably linked to sickness of mind and body. By contrast, we could call Kate's excessive and unrepressed love for her dead husband a *wild* love. Indeed, Kate has let Elnora be wild, much as she has protected the land by not cultivating it, simply allowing it to be. Later we learn that her apparent neglect has had the same effect on her money. Refusing to spend (even on her daughter's school needs) because she assumed she was always on the edge of financial ruin, Kate leaves her deposits to grow untended and they unexpectedly flourish. Elnora might not admit it but she follows the same principle in her romance: she insists on letting her beau go, to be sure he is choosing her freely. This is not just melodramatic convention; she treats him like wild nature.

Wild nature, though, is being frayed away over the course of the story. At the moment Elnora recognizes the need for more natural specimens to sell to pay for graduation expenses, she finds that

the swamp was broken by several graven roads . . . and the machinery of oil wells . . . Wherever the trees fell the moisture dried, the creeks ceased to flow, the river ran low, and at times the bed was dry. With unbroken sweep the winds of the west came, gathering force with every mile and howled and raved; threatening to tear the shingles from the roof, blowing the surface from the soil in clouds of fine dust and rapidly changing everything. . . . butterflies became scarce in proportion to the flowers, while no land yields over three crops of Indian relics.

Elnora's scruples about "collecting" versus "gathering" are ultimately outweighed by the imperative to tell the world what's being lost. Loss in turn necessitates collecting the rarities of the wild to preserve them in books and teaching collections.

This, too, was Stratton-Porter's own mission. She presents the reader with jewels of life-forms and lifeways being lost. More world builder than plotter, she lets characters like Pete Corson and Freckles, the Swamp Angel and the Bird Woman slip in and out, existing in their own world of which we catch but a glimpse, with no fussy summary of previous episodes to fill us in.

Even William Lyon Phelps could not withhold grudging admiration for Stratton-Porter's acquaintance with "every bug, bird, and beast in the woods"; she "lives in a swamp," he wrote, "arrays herself in man's clothes, and sallies forth in all weathers to study the secrets of nature." By knitting ecological fable together with sentimental romance, Stratton-Porter created an unexpectedly haunting tale, resonant with ethical questions still posed today: What is the human duty of care to the world around us? What is the difference between waste and wildness? When neither option can any longer be considered pure, how do we decide between intervention and letting things be?

Chapter Two

THE YOUNG VISITERS

DAISY ASHFORD

CALEB CRAIN

"**MR SALTEENA** was an elderly man of 42 and was fond of asking peaple to stay with him." So begins *The Young Visiters; or, Mr Salteenas Plan*, a comic novel about a social climber who loses the woman he loves. It was written in 1890, when its author, Daisy Ashford, was nine.

There are two obvious ways for a child's novel to be funny. First: naively, by reminding the adult reader of what a child does not know. Every forty-two-year-old knows he isn't *elderly*—while remaining aware, uncomfortably, that to the nine-year-old still inside of him, he catastrophically is.

"He had quite a young girl staying with him of 17 named Ethel Monticue," runs Ashford's next sentence. Here is the second way for a child's novel to be funny: sharply, by revealing how much a child does know, after all. A nine-year-old may not be able to put into words everything that is involved when a forty-two-year-old man lives with a seventeen-year-old girl who isn't related to him. But in the matter of Mr Salteena and Ethel Monticue's life together, Ashford knows even if she can't say—which, for a novelist's purposes, may be the most congenial way of knowing.

What makes *The Young Visiters* exceptional rather than merely entertaining is that in addition to naiveté and cunning, Ashford has a third way of being funny, all her own. It's a fortified strain of free indirect discourse, the literary technique of allowing a narrator's voice to dip into and out of the consciousnesses of a novel's characters. Ashford's lack of quotation marks removes a usual barrier between consciousnesses, and her phonetic spellings establish further links among them. For example, when Ashford writes, of Ethel, that "She had a blue velvit frock which had grown rarther short in the sleeves," the sharing is audible in the spelling *rarther*. The reader can't tell if the qualification is Ashford's or Ethel's, but it isn't, in any case, the way the word is ordinarily written. Maybe it's a qualification that Mr Salteena has made to *his* perception of Ethel's sleeve length? The exact attribution matters much less than the flavor the word gives of a shared way of seeing the world, in which people praise homes as "sumpshous," deliver their more pointed compliments in "rarther a socierty tone," or describe an impressive mantelpiece as "hung with the painting of a lady in a low neck looking quite the thing."

A silly world, in other words—a world where everyone is either preening themselves on their status or scheming to acquire more of it; a world where no one seems to be interested enough in other people, in and for themselves, to be capable of receiving any serious harm at their hands. The satire is accordingly ruthless. "One grows weary of Court Life," sighs the Prince of Wales during a levee he is holding in Buckingham Palace, at which the prince learns that Mr Salteena longs for nothing so much as the chance to "gallopp beside the royal baroushe."

The action of the novel is launched when a friend invites Mr Salteena to visit his country house. The invitation arrives accompanied by the gift of a top hat, and maybe, in late Victorian England, gentlemen were not in fact in the habit of sending top hats when they sent invitations, but who cares, because Mr Salteena's reaction to the top hat is realism of a higher order:

> Then Mr S. opened the box and there lay the most splendid top hat of a lovly rich tone rarther like grapes with a ribbon round compleat.
>
> Well said Mr Salteena peevishly I dont know if I shall like it the bow of the ribbon is too flighty for my age.

Dialogue cannot be made more revelatory of character. "I am not quite a gentleman," Mr Salteena writes, in accepting the invitation, "but you would hardly notice it but cant be helped anyhow." Ashford makes no bones about it: in the world he inhabits, Mr Salteena is doomed and, what's more, deserves his fate. But, with magisterial cruelty, Ashford is just as clear-eyed about the pathos of his ridiculous humanity.

Skepticism about marital bliss came naturally to Ashford. Her maternal grandparents were famously unhappy with each other. It was family lore that one day, when her grandmother came to breakfast in a low-cut gown, her grandfather commented, "I see, my dear, that you have appeared in a state of seminudity which, during the course of the day will, no doubt, become total." He died young and unregretted.

The daughter of this ill-sorted union, Daisy's mother, became engaged to a peer at age twenty-one and then eloped with a coronet, who took her to Ireland, went bankrupt several times over, gave her two daughters and three sons, and died of tuberculosis. Her plight loosened a stipend of a thousand pounds a year from her cranky father's estate, and once she returned to England, at age thirty-eight, her parish priest set her up with a shy, musical forty-four-year-old named Willie Ashford. The man had been living with his mother for sixteen years, in the house where Charles Dickens had written *Nicholas Nickleby*, and though he had once worked in the War Office, he had resigned a decade earlier, for reasons never explained, and was short on funds. On the day of their wedding, the youngish widow wrote in her diary, "Willie looked as tho' he were on to a good thing, as no doubt he was." On their honeymoon they had to pawn his gold watch.

The happy couple quickly added three daughters to the five children from the widow's first marriage. The mother read Dickens aloud to the children, "skipping the dull passages," Ashford's niece reports. Daisy was the eldest of the new daughters and showed an early talent for storytelling. At age four, she dictated the fictional biography of a Jesuit priest who was a family friend. When she and her two sisters played dolls, they did so with a Dickensian appreciation of social hierarchy; the sisters' dolls were understood to be aristocrats and Daisy's to be "mere," the family word for working-class.

The Young Visiters, which Daisy wrote in her own hand, was her third work of fiction and was followed by three more, written at the ages of eleven, twelve, and fourteen. No one thought of publishing them at the time, but her mother salted them away, and in 1917, after her mother's death, Ashford found them again in a box of mementos. She was by then thirty-five and, still single, running a canteen in Dover as her contribution to the war effort. She showed *The Young Visiters* to her sisters, who laughed over it, and then loaned it for amusement's sake to a literary friend who had come down with the flu. The friend, once recovered, read a chapter aloud after dinner one night while on a country house visit. It so happened that an editor from Chatto & Windus was also a guest; he bought the rights and recruited J. M. Barrie, the author of *Peter Pan*, to write an introduction.

The Young Visiters went on to sell about half a million copies over the course of the twentieth century. "I can never feel all the nice things that have been said about 'The Young Visiters' are really due to me at all, but to a Daisy Ashford of so long ago that she seems another person," Ashford wrote in 1920.

She burned the only manuscript she is known to have written as an adult. The brilliance of *The Young Visiters* was a piece of unrepeatable, inexplicable luck, as any successful novel written by a child has to be—and as most successful novels written by adults probably are as well. The luck in this case had to do with how well the child's frankness described adult vulnerabilities, such as the essentially childish weakness of poking at a lover's vanity when in danger of losing her.

"You will look very silly," Ashford imagines Mr Salteena telling Ethel as Ethel considers putting on rouge for a trip that the two are planning.

Well so will you said Ethel in a snappy tone and she ran out of the room with a very superier run throwing out her legs behind and her arms swinging in rithum.

Well said the owner of the house she has a most idiotick run.

About the sort of bad habits that are never outgrown, a child already knows everything there is to know.

Chapter Three

THE DIARY OF "HELENA MORLEY"

ELIZABETH BISHOP, TRANS.

ELIZABETH FERRY

ON NOVEMBER 26, 1893, a thirteen-year-old Anglo-Brazilian girl opens her diary to record a rescue mission. Helena's father, a diamond miner in Diamantina, in Minas Gerais, Brazil, has gone to Biribiri, about twenty kilometers away, to check out a new mine. One afternoon, his mule shows up at home, waiting to be fed. "We must get ready to leave early tomorrow morning. Something's happened to Alexandre," says Helena's mother, tears in her eyes. The next day she wakes Helena and her siblings for their trek: "Get up! The rooster's already crowed twice! It must be 4 o'clock."

They set out. After a long time, they hear a church bell strike two and realize their mother has forgotten (and not for the first time) that roosters sometimes crow all night. They keep walking under the stars but soon grow anxious about the road. Finally, her mother calls a halt: "This road is really too strange. We'd better sit down and wait for daylight." Helena continues her story with a characteristic flair for the dramatic: "When it was daylight, what an abyss! . . . It was the very top of the Serra dos Cristais and from up there we saw the road far below. We were on a precipice!"

That tiny sliver of a story contains the quintessence of *The Diary of "Helena Morley,"* first published, in 1942, as *Minha vida de menina* (My life as a young girl), by its author, Alice Dayrell—who borrowed the pseudonym "Helena Morley" from her father's side of the family. Its freshness and precision in depicting late nineteenth-century provincial mining life quickly made it a hit in Brazil, as did the determined promotional efforts of the exiled French novelist Georges Bernanos. By the 1950s, copies were apparently presented every year as "prize books" to students of Rio's Convent of the Sacred Heart.

It was, however, something more than Brazilian antiquarianism that drew the American poet Elizabeth Bishop to translate it. She was intoxicated by the sense, as she writes, that "*it really happened* . . . day by day, minute by minute, once and only once." The book as we have it in English, with Bishop's own incisive and vivid introduction, keeps that sense of real happening alive.

By the time Bishop met "Dona Alice," the latter was a respected lady of seventy-six years old and "very much a matriarch," wife of the director of the Bank of Brazil. She and her husband showed Bishop poignant memorabilia: a letter from George Bernanos, earlier versions of the book, photographs. Bishop even learned that in 1867, the English explorer Sir Richard Burton had met Alice's father in Diamantina and written about him in his *Explorations of the Highlands of the*

Brazil. He was, writes Bishop, "even then at work mining diamonds, as he is later, throughout the pages of his daughter's
diary." To me, "even then at work mining diamonds" captures
the sense of overlapping past and present, so vividly present
throughout the diary. And "throughout the pages of his daughter's diary" evokes the diary as a landscape in which Alice and her
family are still working, playing, squabbling, and celebrating.

Bishop was right—the book breathes actuality, with its
high- and lowlights. Over here, the chancy nature of diamond
mining: after Alice's friend Arinda discovers a "really big diamond," her uncle "gave Arinda five brand-new hundred *mil reis*
notes. She ran off to her father's cabin with all of us after her.
Her father, her mother and everyone was crazy with joy. Her
father folded up the bills and put them in his pocket, took
them out again and looked at them, and put them back again."
Over there, the complacent racism of these years just after the
end of slavery: "I don't know why one of [the biracial girls living nearby] turned out to be white and pretty. . . . She married
a Negro who is so ugly it breaks your heart. . . . On the wedding day, papa said, 'It's throwing pearls before swine.' Everybody was sorry."

On the last page of Laura Ingalls Wilder's *Little House in the
Big Woods*, Laura says to herself as she falls asleep, "Now is
now. It can never be a long time ago." That realization about
the unapproachability of the past is not just the young Laura's.
It also belongs to the writer of those sentences, already an old
woman. Also to Wilder's silent collaborator, her daughter,
Rose, gazing back at those far-off inaccessible memories. And
finally it even belongs to the book's readers, yet more removed.

The poignancy of *The Diary of "Helena Morley"* also lies in its double life: both vivid presence and distant memory.

Bishop reveled in that doubleness: her introduction details her own impulse to seek out, in Morley's words and in her town, a past that is both immediate and unrecapturable. Not satisfied to meet "Helena," she also roamed Diamantina searching for signs of the past: "Some of the people in the diary are still alive, and the successors of those who are dead and gone seem very much cut from the same cloth. Little uniformed girls, with perhaps shorter skirts, carrying satchels of books, press their noses against the dining-room windows of the new hotel and are overcome with fits of giggling at seeing the foreigner eat her lunch."

Gazing out at these little schoolgirls, Bishop feels something more than pathos. There is a pleasingly contrived quality to this double exposure, like some ingenious contraption at the fair—a sensation of delight, as well as nostalgia, in the way a younger generation stands in for a bygone one.

This desire to experience the bygone as present doesn't stop: as I reread the book recently, it brought back the time when I first read it, in 1998, in a mining town in Mexico, watching schoolchildren clatter down a cobblestone road and drinking punch with hawthorn berries during evening Advent processions. Books, like places, are never the same twice. Yet that never stops us trying to spin the clock backward, to make the time machine operate as promised, just this once.

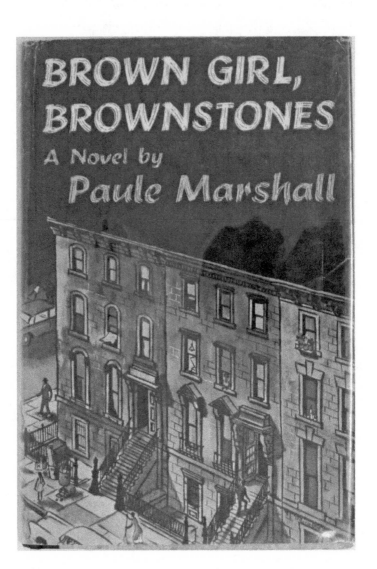

BROWN GIRL, BROWNSTONES

A Novel by

Paule Marshall

Chapter Four

BROWN GIRL, BROWNSTONES

PAULE MARSHALL: IN MEMORIAM

ADRIENNE BROWN

Paule Marshall, MacArthur and Guggenheim fellow and the author of such celebrated novels as *The Chosen Place, The Timeless People* and *Praiseong for the Widow,* passed away in August 2019, at the age of 90. When invited to write in memoriam, Adrienne Brown unhesitatingly chose Marshall's first novel, *Brown Girl, Brownstones.*

THE JULY 1960 issue of *Esquire*—dedicated to New York—featured consecutive essays by the writers John Cheever and James Baldwin. "Moving Out" features Cheever grappling with his decision to leave the city for good; he ends by proclaiming himself "crazy about the suburbs." Baldwin's "Fifth Avenue, Uptown," a sobering counterpoint, sketches contained and constricted black populations: "The people in Harlem know they are living there because white people do not think they are good enough to live anywhere else." Baldwin links Harlem's ongoing stagnation to Cheever's "evacuation."

Both Cheever's and Baldwin's cognitive maps, though, omit the small Brooklyn enclave of Barbadian immigrants that features in Paule Marshall's remarkable first novel, *Brown Girl, Brownstones* (1959). Cheever and Baldwin depict New York as a place of stark divide; Marshall captures complex and confusing overlappings that collectively make and unmake her young Black protagonist, Selina Boyce. Coming of age (as Marshall herself did) within the Barbadian Brooklyn community in the 1940s and '50s, Selina experiences a New York continually quivering under the crisscrossed and ever-moving lines—lines of color but also class, gender, nationality, sexuality, and age, a cat's cradle Selina must learn to maneuver. In that, her family is both obstacle and resource.

I first read *Brown Girl, Brownstones* as a first-year Ph.D. student. At twenty-one, only a little older than Selina is at the novel's end, I related to her desire to forge a self that was more than just reactively oppositional to the world of her upbringing. Selina eventually manages this by traveling to the Caribbean of her parent's origin, a place she has never been. My own strategy was to turn my youthful alienations into intellectual pursuits. I arrived at graduate school wondering why the diverse lower-income suburb from which I had hailed did not resemble those that John Cheever loved and James Baldwin reproached. I felt a deep connection to Selina's story. More surprising, though, was everything Marshall's novel of Bajan immigrants had to say about the suburbs as a site reshaping race at midcentury. How did the tropes for describing the suburbs first emerge, and what work did they do? Answering that question would prove central to my academic life.

Although the word *suburb* never appears, *Brown Girl, Brownstone* proves much better at evoking the longing that produced the suburbs than much of the literature actually set there. For one, Marshall renders white flight as something more akin to white haunting and hanging on. In an inversion of the creole Bertha Mason locked away upstairs in *Jane Eyre*, Selina's family is haunted by the attic-dwelling Mary and her daughter, Maritze, remainders from the neighborhood's earlier era of white occupation. (They are, however, "white" only viewed against dark backdrop of their Barbadian neighbors; in the eyes the pedigreed and Protestant society members they once served, their ethnicity and their Catholicism had always constituted an insurmountable barrier). Maritze aims to secure her whiteness once and for all by purchasing one of the "inexpensive houses on Long Island" where "every decent white person's moving away, getting out." Even as the novel focuses on Selina's coming into her own amid the hard and tender world of New York, it gestures toward how suburbia was remaking white womanhood simultaneously.

What goes around comes around. As Selina grows up, it becomes increasingly ironic to her that the Bajan families around her, despite being looked down by the Maritzes of the world as "black foreign scum," largely seek to replicate Maritze's own formula for advancement. With the suburbs out of reach, her parent's generation longs to own homes in Crown Heights, exploiting African Americans as renters in order to afford this prize. "We would like to do different," Selina's mother laments, "but the way things arrange we can't, if not we lose out."

Selina fiercely holds out for an alternative: "It was her own small truth that dimly envisioned a different world and a different way; a small belief—illusory and undefined still—which was slowly forming out of all she had lived." The contours of that different world start to take shape as Selina enters college in Manhattan, where she encounters people and art unlike anything of her childhood.

Her hopes of challenging "the way things arrange," though, soon collapse. After performing an inspired dance solo, Selina is cut down to size by the mother of a white classmate. Surprised to learn that Selina hails from Brooklyn rather than Harlem, the woman grills her about her Caribbean heritage before comparing Selina to a "girl" from the islands who once worked for her. The bitter Maritze of Selina's childhood looked to the suburbs to attain whiteness. By contrast, this woman belittles Selina to assure herself of the remaining force her whiteness still wields in the city—even as her peers (think of John Cheever) are rapidly leaving for greener pastures.

As a grad student, I eagerly studied Marshall's descriptions of the changing contours of whiteness at midcentury. However, *Brown Girl, Brownstones* is equally devoted to capturing the intricacies of Black becoming within a largely Black world. We first meet Selina and her family before the war in 1939 as the "uniform red-brown stone" of the neighborhood's similar homes belies the tumultuous agon of their specific residence. Selina and her sister weather the fierce battles waged between their elegant, idle, and increasingly broken father and their sharp-tongued, willful, and differently injured mother. Selina clings to her father while resisting "the mother," as the novel refers to her, whom Selina simultaneously adores, identifies with, and loathes.

Marshall depicts Selina's family members harming one another in unforgiveable ways, injuries all the more painful because they come from a place of voracious love. The shocking sting of Selina experience with that classmate's mother comes late in the novel. By that juncture, she already feels so smothered by the world of her family and her block that she viscerally rejects its norms and desires without fully understanding the injuries and oppressions driving her community's obsession with advancement. Only when she experiences this sort of racial injury can she glimpse how deeply that pain has maimed her own parents.

The hurtful alienation existing between Selina and her parents was (and remains) a marvel to me, a revelation. But the novel's minor characters are equally memorable. The limping Mrs. Thompson and lustful Suggie guide Selina into womanhood; Selina's childhood best friend, Beryl, never stops believing in her even as their worldviews increasingly diverge. Then there is Clive, the dreamy Black bohemian painter with whom Selina has her first love affair. Writers at midcentury generally rendered Black male bohemians as pitiful sell-outs or farcically effete—see Amiri Baraka's *Dutchman* (1964). But Marshall draws Clive just as richly as Selina. Disillusioned with "the whole pathetic Village scene," Clive suffers from "seeing things in my mind that I can't get down right on canvas."

Of course, as idle and sad bohemians are wont to do, Clive ultimately breaks Selina's heart. But he loves Selina without jealously or violence for all that she is. This is not the tortured love of Janie Crawford (in Zora Neal Hurston's *Their Eyes Were Watching God* [1937]) or the melancholic toleration of Gwendolyn Brooks's Maud Martha (1953). Clive and Selina's love fizzles out because he doesn't know how to give her what she wants and she doesn't yet know what that is exactly. But the ordinariness of these young Black lovers' coming together and falling apart is part of what makes the novel feel so radiant.

Like Toni Morrison nearly a decade later, Paule Marshall penned her *Brown Girl, Brownstones* at night, fitting it in around her day job as a magazine writer. But the debut novels of these two writers about Black girlhood in America could not be more different. The marigolds refused to grow in Morrison's *The Bluest Eye* (1970). Where Morrison depicts a Black girl dreadfully longing for the alleged beauty of whiteness, Marshall's protagonist leaves the United States to seek an alternative to its deadlocked cycles of racial injury. We need both of these portraits, and many more. Brown girls can navelgaze, find themselves through modern dance, and fall in love with dashingly wounded painters. *Brown Girl, Brownstones* proved that such journeys—so precious to their protagonists yet also so everyday, so ordinary—had a vital place in the Black experience. Even if they weren't yet marked on anyone else's map.

Chapter Five

AN AMERICAN CHILDHOOD

ANNIE DILLARD

SALVATORE SCIBONA

I FIRST read it as a teenager in Cleveland, Ohio, sitting on a concrete wharf by Lake Erie with the interstate at my back; sitting on a bench in the hardwood forest of a county park; walking on suburban sidewalks by pizza joints and strip malls. I couldn't understand the effect it had on me. I felt both exhilarated and irrelevant, awake, free of self, present with my surroundings. The book told of a deeper world inside the atoms of anything the mind perceived.

I stopped on the sidewalk and reread a page while the cars passed. I kept walking, stopped, thought, and read the page again. My mind became the page. Twenty-four years later I see that the teenager who felt at one with this book understood it only obscurely; all the same, he was alive to it in a way the adult mind can never replicate. We grow egos in order to save ourselves from upheavals like this.

An American Childhood (originally published in 1987, when Dillard was forty-two) is about the coming-into-being of consciousness. If a memoir is a record of events as filtered through the author's memory, it's safe to call this a memoir, but its narrative intelligence doesn't feel like an ego testifying to its adventures. Dillard remains in the background in deference to the Pittsburgh of the 1950s and '60s—a subject both specific and rangy enough to contain jazz, jokes, the technique of a joke, the results of the French and Indian War, her mother's skin and clothes, church manners, baseball, dances, nuns who roll footlessly like tanks, streetcars, rock collections, and the Allegheny and Monongahela Rivers, which meet at Pittsburgh and form the "westward-wending Ohio." The author's name appears nowhere in the text.

Dillard struggles to conform her mind to the material world that is its natural subject, but over the course of the narrative, adolescent self-consciousness emerges to bedevil and stymie her.

> I had been transparent to myself, unselfconscious, learning, doing, most of every day. Now I was in my own way; I myself was a dark object I could not ignore. I couldn't remember how to forget myself. I didn't want to think about myself, to reckon myself in, to deal with myself every livelong minute on top of everything else—but swerve as I might, I couldn't avoid it. I was a boulder blocking my own path. I was a dog barking between my own ears.

After adolescence, we probably never stop being self-conscious, except while we sleep. But when we speak of "feeling" self-conscious we underscore a special anguish, an acute aware-ness of our separateness. Nothing could be further from Freud's indelible description, in *Civilization and Its Discontents*, of an infant perceiving itself as undifferentiated from the world: a sense adults recall as something limitless, "oceanic." Later on, the infant won't so much discover the world outside as construct it by erecting a wall across a previously unbounded conscious-ness. According to Freud, the ego "separates off an external world from itself." Because we know that we are also part of the world, we suffer the further anguish of having exiled ourselves *from ourselves*.

Dillard's homesickness for Pittsburgh doubles as a home-sickness for the unselfconscious mind of childhood, which she can only observe now at a distance, sequestered in a pine shed on Cape Cod, an adult writer "concentrating, lost in the past." She half believes she can hear her mother coming across the grass—only to wake and "break up through the skin of aware-ness a thousand times a day, as dolphins burst through seas." Dillard's narrator is not an ego but the "I" of the transcenden-talists, possessing knowledge it has come by from realms beyond the physical: "The poems whispered in my ear the password phrase, and I memorized it behind enemy lines: There is a world. There is another world." Dillard's mind para-doxically digs into itself to get *out*, as through a wormhole, into the world of beetles, ferns, minerals: the physical things charged with numinous meaning that would become the sub-ject of her later work.

Dillard regards this struggle to free ourselves from self-consciousness as a tension elemental to the species, immune from cure. The mature mind therefore has to come to some accommodation to make all this knowingness worthwhile. And the bravura passages of the book—both analytically incisive and sweeping in their music—are the long metaphors through which she surveys this dilemma. She describes the adult "I" looking at the world as at a map.

"When everything else has gone from my brain," she writes on the first page, "what will be left, I believe, is topology: the dreaming memory of land as it lay this way and that." Sad to have to say "topology" rather than "Pittsburgh," but that is exactly the problem: the adult knows the logos of the place better than the place itself. Even when everything else has left her brain, she will revert not to the infant's oneness with the place but to the adult's study of it.

Our exile from childhood is permanent—yet *An American Childhood* avoids being a sentimental celebration of lost innocence. In Dillard's reckoning, the emotional effect of our ability to be in the world *and know it* is finally not despair but rejoicing and gratitude.

If you notice unbidden that you are afoot on this particular mountain on this particular day in the company of these particular changing fragments of clouds,— if you pause in your daze to connect your own skull-locked and interior mumble with the skin of your senses and sense, and notice you are living,—then will you not conjure up in imagination a map or a globe and locate this low mountain ridge on it, and find on one western slope the dot which represents you walking here astonished?

What is important is anyone's coming awake and discovering a place, finding in full orbit a spinning globe one can lean over, catch, and jump on. What is important is the moment of opening a life and feeling it touch—with an electric hiss and cry—this speckled mineral sphere, our present world.

Self-consciousness may have separated us from the world, but it is also our most robust remaining connection with the world. "Your very cells have been replaced," but you still have access to the oldest of sensations, like the one that happens when you lower your foot into a hot bath: "You feel the chill spread inside your shoulders, shoot down your arms and rise to your lips." What matters, the book concludes, "is the dizzying overreal sensation of noticing that you are here."

This feeling of "noticing you are here" may echo the infant's old oceanic one, but the two will never be the same. The infant knew neither "I" nor "here"—nor the shortness of life, such that we will later prize just a moment of illumination among the dwindling years. A foot in a bath. A book that stops your heart and seems to know what your mind is for.

Chapter Six

THE LAST SAMURAI

HELEN DEWITT

TORIL MOI

GENIUS, GAMES, languages, alphabets. The wonders and the cruelty of the world. The poverty and loneliness of the authentic artist. And underneath the games always the question: Is existence worth enduring?

Formally, Helen DeWitt's *The Last Samurai* is a potent brew of old-fashioned storytelling, high-wire modernist interior monologue, and postmodernism: its experimental layout includes capital letters, broken-off sentences, lists of numbers, and words in many different alphabets. Central to the novel is the metaphor of games, mostly in the sense of games of skill and chance (bridge, piquet). A game of skill is a free yet rule-governed activity: we enter into it willingly, yet once inside its rules bind us. Like the French Oulipo writers (who set themselves mad tasks: compose a novel without the letter *e*!), DeWitt is fascinated by creativity voluntarily imposing strict yet random rules on it.

The Last Samurai opens with the travails of Sibylla. Born
into a long line of unrecognized geniuses, she has made her
way from the American Midwest to a research fellowship in
classics at Oxford. When she discovers that academia fails to
value the difference between mindless learning and true intel-
lect, she decamps. A one-night stand with a smug and self-
important writer (she only had sex with him because she
couldn't find a polite way to say no) results in her son, Ludo,
whose name, not coincidentally, means "I play" in Latin. Sibylla's socioeconomic isolation and the extreme boredom of
having to earn her living typing and tagging text from magazines with titles like *Advanced Angling* and *The Poodle Breeder*
make her depressed. She begins to lecture Ludo on the rational advantages of suicide.

A demanding child, Ludo pesters his brilliant mother to
teach him Greek, Japanese, and mathematics. By the age of
four, he watches Kurosawa's film *The Seven Samurai* almost as
compulsively as Sibylla does. To escape their cold apartment,
Sibylla and Ludo ride the London Underground's Circle line
for whole days on end. This exposes them to wildly uncompre-
hending questioning from their fellow passengers and condemns
poor Sibylla to staying up half the night to type *Practical
Caravanning*.

In part 2, the five-year-old Ludo begins to write a diary. The
novel now begins to shift the perspective away from Sibylla's
consciousness to Ludo's. By part 3, we mostly hear Ludo's
voice. I take this to mean that Sibylla is slowly losing her voice,
slowly becoming mute. When he turns six, Ludo's diary chronicles his encounter with the curiosity-killing school system,

which can only conceive of him as a disruptive influence. This so infuriates Sibylla that she decides to educate him herself. In a way, Ludo becomes the work of art or scholarship Sibylla is too depressed to write.

And what a piece of art he is! At eleven, this thoughtful and kind child genius sets out to find his father. He discovers right away that his biological father is the despicable Val Peters, a successful but sexist and self-aggrandizing travel writer. Like Sibylla before him, Ludo simply can't bring himself to tell this vain and stupid man that he has a son. Instead, he sets off on a search for a more admirable father. In DeWitt's novel, elective affinities beat biological families every time.

In Kurosawa's *Seven Samurai* the first samurai, Kambei, auditions others to join him. In the same way, Ludo interviews potential fathers: an explorer, a popular astronomer, a visual artist, a competitive cardplayer. So the novel begins to widen out; no longer stuck on the Circle line, the reader gets to hear panoramic stories of travels, languages, discoveries, cruelty, and pain. These episodes are paeans to the power of human curiosity and the love of knowledge.

In the end, however, all the father candidates fall short of Ludo's requirements. They may be brilliant, but they have insufferable flaws, mostly connected to their craving for fame and recognition. They are vain or self-promoting or slightly corrupt or just too enamored of public glory. Ludo's quest for a father appears to end when the most promising father figure (Red Devlin, a human rights reporter) kills himself in Ludo's presence. Trained by Sibylla to respect suicide as a perfectly rational response to the evils of the world, Ludo understands his choice. Yet he finds himself wondering: Why can't he bear the thought of Sibylla doing the same thing?

To save Sibylla, Ludo sets out on one last quest. When he was only five, Sibylla took Ludo to a concert by a young experimental Japanese pianist, Kenzo Yamamoto. The eleven-hour concert affected her so deeply that she entirely forgot that she even had a son. Ludo walked home alone while Sibylla sat as if bewitched, overcome by the sense that Yamamoto's music spoke directly to her life: "There is only one chance at life once gone it is gone for good you must seize the moments before it goes, tears were streaming down my face as I heard these three pieces each with just one chance of being heard."

Still only twenty-five, Yamamoto has long since stopped performing. Ludo, now thirteen, seeks him out and claims, implausibly enough, to be his son. To forestall objections he begins speaking Toshirō Mifune's lines from the scene in *Seven Samurai* in which Mifune's character, Kikuchiyo, produces a certificate to prove that he is a real samurai. But, as Kambei points out, according to the document this grown man is only thirteen years old. Yet, in the end, Kambei still welcomes Kikuchiyo. In the same way, Yamamoto begins to speak Kambei's lines, welcoming Ludo into his life. More than that, he lets Ludo persuade him to record a CD that just might inspire Sibylla to find a way to express her own genius.

The Last Samurai is at once playful and deeply serious, a masterly blend of tragedy and comedy; the reader both sinks into Sibylla's dark despair and stretches up toward the light with Ludo. Impossible to summarize (each character opens up a world), it is deeply political—anticapitalist and thoroughly feminist—without ever becoming preachy or moralizing.

It's difficult, in fact, to imagine a less politically correct feminist writer than DeWitt. As evidence I submit her ironic, sly, funny, and deeply political parable *Lightning Rods* (2011), in which a vacuum cleaner salesman called Joe invents a surefire way to protect large companies against sexual harassment suits: hire women to do ordinary office jobs in the company but at double the salary, given that they will also work as anonymous "lightning rods." Joe has patented an ingenious contraption that lets the lower half of a woman's body slide through the wall into a cubicle in the men's toilet, so that the man can relieve himself sexually without knowing who the "lightning rod" is. To assure anonymity the woman's lower half is clad in black latex with a strategically placed slit. As a result, workplace morale increases, and some of the lightning rods earn enough to fund their college educations and go on to have brilliant careers. Written well before the #MeToo movement, *Lightning Rods* is a modern *Candide*, a brilliant satire of the mechanisms of capitalism in a patriarchal society.

DeWitt's theme of unacknowledged genius up against the harsh realities of the late capitalist marketplace is on full display in *Some Trick*, her 2018 short story collection. A musician leaves his band; another commits suicide; a sublime piano player retires young; an artist gets swindled by her gallerist; and a mathematician despairs at his inability to make his agent listen. DeWitt's villains are usually art bureaucrats—gallery owners, agents, editors, and other denizens of the "art world," who are only too ready to "love" writers they haven't read and to travesty the artist's vision in order to make money off her creativity. Meanwhile the artist is left high and dry, unacknowledged and unpaid.

Nevertheless, for me, *The Last Samurai* remains DeWitt's masterpiece. I read it as a contemporary rewrite of Mme de Staël's *Corinne, or Italy* (1807). In de Staël's novel the female genius is crowned and acclaimed by the people of Italy but is undone by romantic love. She falls in love with a man who cannot conceive of a wife who performs in public. Corinne, who in one scene dresses like the ancient Roman Sibyl, loses her voice, her powers of expression, and dies from a broken heart.

In DeWitt's world, women of genius never find romantic love. Like Sibylla, they encounter only awkward sexual situations. Whereas Corinne is surrounded by admirers, Sibylla is all alone. Her responsibility toward her astonishing son has kept her alive, but in DeWitt's novel motherhood alone is not a reason for living. Just as Corinne's death stands as a judgment on a world that can make no place for a woman like her, Sibylla's depressed and lonely existence expresses DeWitt's withering critique of the destiny of genuine artists and intellectuals in our own world. But at the end of *The Last Samurai*, the future is still open. Maybe Sibylla will find a way out. Maybe Ludo will grow up to flourish. But one thing is certain: unless they can find ways to play, create, and explore, their lives will have no meaning.

PART II

OTHER WORLDS

ARE THE distant worlds that writers invent simply dark mirrors of our own shared actuality? Or are they tickets to elsewhere, reminders that things can be far different from what surrounds us now? Each of these books ventures into an uncertain beyond. Some writers do find a way back from these mysterious other worlds. Seeta Chaganti sees in the "endless knot" of *Gawain and the Green Knight*'s allegorical pentangle a conception of shame that still resonates today. Kate Marshall proposes that the planetary vitality of *Solaris* ("the ocean lived, thought, and acted") means more in the present Anthropocene-aware era than it did when Lem first put pen to paper. And Ivan Kreilkamp praises *Lolly Willowe*'s tale of witchery because Sylvia Townsend Warner "pulls off the difficult feat of making English respectability seem dangerously revolutionary."

Other writers, though, keep gazing outward, letting readers feel alien all the way down. Namwali Serpell rescues William

Hope Hodgson's *The House on the Borderlands* from more than a century of near-oblivion because Hodgson reminds readers "just how uneasily we sit within the endless spinning of time." In the strange journey that the protagonist of *Other Leopards* takes back through millennia to meet the "Queen of Time," Emily Hyde sees Dennis William staging "not an identification with the past as a basis for future development, [but] a repudiation of historical time." The religious historian Katie Lofton recalls the sublime displacements of childhood when she discovered in Edith Hamilton's myths "cockeyed desires [that] strung together risk and longing, manipulation and capture. Part of the thrill was not knowing what role I wanted for myself in the story." And Paul Saint-Amour finds that Russell Hoban's language-coining *Riddley Walker* "mak[es] us feel spectral in the midst of life; it confronts us with a posterity that looks back at us blankly as we peer at it."

Chapter Seven

SIR GAWAIN AND THE GREEN KNIGHT

SEETA CHAGANTI

IF YOU last read *Sir Gawain and the Green Knight* long ago, you might mainly remember the striking and supernatural image of a huge green warrior riding away from King Arthur's court, his hand clutching his own severed head. To many scholars, though, this is a poem less about magic than about shame and guilt. At the court, Gawain and his comrades endure the shame of being called out publicly by the green stranger, and private pangs of guilt rack the virtuous knight when he fails to measure up to trials and temptations.

Such preoccupations may make the poem seem particularly arcane and irrelevant right now. Under Donald Trump, shame, guilt, and honor seem long vanished from even the rearview mirror; shamelessness reigns. Yet *Sir Gawain*'s very emphasis on shame can teach us a lesson about that shamelessness: its harm lies not only in the havoc that the shameless can wreak but also in the possibility that when a powerful person casts off shame, it lodges itself within those who would resist him.

Shame influences Sir Gawain's story from the outset. The Green Knight appears at Camelot with a challenge: strike me with an axe, in return for which you must present yourself at my chapel in a year and a day to receive the same treatment. After some hesitation, Gawain agrees and decapitates the mysterious figure, hoping this puts an end to the nonsensical bargain. But he and the court watch in horror as the Green Knight matter-of-factly picks up his own severed head, which pointedly tells Gawain: *See you next year.* Odd as this exchange might seem, it is fundamentally chivalrous, displaying and assuming honorable behavior. Except for one telling fact: Gawain accepts the Green Knight's challenge not with noble alacrity but only because no one else will. Gawain sees Arthur blush, the blood shooting for shame into his shining face. Only then does he step up.

More shame is to come. On the journey to meet the Green Knight a year later, Gawain sojourns in a mysterious castle. There, he agrees to a bargain with Bertilak, the castle's lord: each will give the other what he has received at the end of every day. Bertilak spends his mornings hunting, presenting Gawain on successive days with a deer, a boar, and a fiendish fox. Gawain, meanwhile, remains inside the castle. Here, Bertilak's wife presses kisses upon him, which Gawain daily renders to Bertilak. Both the kissing and its disclosure embarrass Gawain: scholars see this as a milder version of shame but still in that family of experiences.

Something else happens during their game, however, that indicates not shame but its absence. Bertilak's wife offers Gawain a green girdle that she says will protect him. This he agrees to conceal from his host, breaking the terms of his deal with Bertilak. His plan to abscond with the girdle implies that—even if only momentarily—the threat of shame disappears for Gawain. Perhaps cowardice or self-preservation motivates this decision, but it is uncharacteristic and thus raises a crucial question: What has permitted Gawain to act as though shame did not exist?

The poem's answer, I think, is entitlement. When Gawain arrives at Bertilak's castle and explains his errand, his host reassures him that the Green Chapel—the home of the Green Knight—is close by and that Gawain can relax without fear of missing his tryst. Gawain delightedly responds: "My quest is accomplished" ("acheued is my chaunce"). Although he is still two miles from the chapel, the challenges of the intervening days yet unknown, Gawain perceives a done deal. He laughs; it's going to be so easy.

This moment marks a subtle turning point. Immediately afterward, Gawain cheerfully assents to Bertilak's trading game. As a guest he has little choice, but the breeziness of his acquiescence gives pause; does he not recognize that just this type of trading got him in trouble before, when the Green Knight proposed it? Deluded that he has achieved something he has not, Gawain feels emboldened to ignore consequences. In that state of mind, shamelessness becomes possible, and it rears its head when Gawain decides to conceal the girdle.

The Trump era has shown us how powerful people exaggerate their successes while refusing to exhibit shame at their moral failures. *Sir Gawain* cuts through local details of politics, psychology, and incompetence to anatomize this shamelessness at its most stylized and elemental. When encouraged to feel entitled, even the most spotlessly honorable knight can lose all sense of shame. Imagine how much easier the slide for someone longer on entitlement and shorter on honorable standards.

The poem proceeds to suggest that once you shrug off shame, your relationship to it is forever tenuous. Even though Gawain goes on to display shame, the exhibition is confusing. The Green Knight (none other than Bertilak in disguise) confronts Gawain with his ignoble act—that is, concealing the girdle—when he arrives at the Green Chapel. Gawain shrinks for shame, but this reaction is hardly unalloyed. Not only does Gawain dilute his shame by blaming women for his actions, but the Green Knight also makes excuses for Gawain: You feared for your life, so how can we blame you for your mediocre performance? You are still an exceptional pearl.

Gawain tries to hold onto his shame by proposing that he will now wear the girdle as a band of his blame. But his peers insist on treating his shame as a marker of worth. The court adopts the girdle, the very token he proposes to wear as a signal of his permanent stain, as a badge of honor. Perhaps Gawain remains ashamed. But the poem declines to depict this: it expands outward and away from Gawain, invoking, in its final lines, King Arthur, the Trojan War, and Christ. Once Gawain has opened up the possibility of rejecting shame, the poem can end by relinquishing red-faced emotional specificity in favor of the obfuscating sweep of history.

When shame's location is obscured, does it disappear entirely? The medieval text holds unique potential to explore this question. We know *Sir Gawain* because it survives in a manuscript, a handwritten copy. Medieval manuscripts are often inscribed not only with the text in question but also with ancillary comments and additions. *Sir Gawain* is no exception: after the poem's ending, someone has jotted the motto of the Order of the Garter, *"Honi soit qui mal y pense* [Shame on any-one who thinks anything shady is going on here]." This inclusion has been deemed a "curious logic" that turns shame on the observer. Where the ending of the poem cannot locate shame, then, the manuscript's embellishment can: shame lands on us, the observers.

In the poem, Gawain's shield is decorated with a pentangle, a five-pointed star. I would suggest that we can understand this device as illustrating the motion of shame as well as its ultimate virulence. As a completed symbol, the pentangle conveys honor and virtue, an "endeles knot." But as the scholar Geraldine Heng notes, the pentangle is also an ambiguous, overdetermined gnarl on which the narrative catches. What, after all, does it mean to draw that knot? It ricochets and lands on different points as you trace it. And once you start drawing the star, it has inexorable momentum. In this sense, the tracery of the pentangle is the moving force of shame: once initiated, it has to exist somewhere. If you reject it, it will continue to bounce and prick in other corners. When an enfranchised pro-tagonist (a knight, a politician) is coddled to cast off shame, that shame becomes a sharp point set loose to lodge collaterally in his watchers.

The Trump administration has driven that sharp point into me. I am pierced by the shame he refuses to feel. I see Trump as merely intensifying what are in fact longstanding injustices and evils; I see myself as accountable for my belatedness in resisting them. And I know that even as I try to do better, I am complicit still. But *Sir Gawain* offers perspective on these disabling anxieties, revealing them as the shame that shamelessness makes its weapon. Perhaps this recognition offers an exit route from that sense of entrapment, regression, and futility, an escape from drawing the pentangle's endless, privileged knot.

Chapter Eight

THE HOUSE ON THE BORDERLAND

WILLIAM HOPE HODGSON

NAMWALI SERPELL

TERRY PRATCHETT'S 1988 summary of *The House on the Border-land* begins: "Man buys House. House attacked Nightly by Horrible Swine Things from Hole in Garden. Man Fights Back with Determination and Lack of Imagination of Political Proportions." It ends: "The journey to the Central Suns sold me infinity." Infinity is a rather lofty reward for persevering through a battle with pig-men. But Pratchett was right. William Hope Hodgson's novel, published in 1908 (but likely written in 1904) is one of the most startling accounts of infinity that I've ever read.

The novel came to me serendipitously: my friend Mike stumbled across it while googling some Dungeons & Dragons thing called "Into the Borderlands." He read it, loved it, and passed it on to me. I read it with no knowledge of who Hodgson was or what I was getting into. As an immigrant, I often experience the delight of belated discovery: Frederick Douglass,

Star Wars, *Lolita*. But with Hodgson, I'm not alone. After his death in Ypres at age forty-one, Hodgson was mostly forgotten until a brief—and apparently unsuccessful—revival in the 1930s.

When fiction reappears after a spell of obscurity, we often say it was before its time. To me, *The House on the Borderland* is untimely in another, more enthralling way: it undoes time. It begins conventionally enough. The narrator (a figure for the author) and his friend decide to take a fishing trip to "a tiny hamlet called Kraighten" in the west of Ireland—an unusual place for a vacation, but a classic frame for a Gothic tale all the same. One day, the two men go exploring. Tracking a strange spray of water shooting up above the canopy, they find themselves in a kind of jungly lowland with a pit in the middle of it. Jutting into this pit is a protruding rock, at the tip of which sits the ruins of an old house. In the rubble, they find a half-destroyed book—a diary. Smoking their pipes at camp that night, "Hodgson" reads it aloud.

The entries feel at first like a haunted-house story, with echoes of Edgar Allan Poe: a rambling old mansion bought by folks from out of town, a canine companion named Pepper who tugs at our heartstrings, intimations of a long-lost love, and a hero unaccountably drawn to investigate holes in the ground. But then the diarist recounts a strange vision of spinning out into the universe and descending upon an unearthly plain ringed with mountains, a black sun limned by a ring of fire hovering over it. In the middle of the amphitheater, he sees what appears to be a replica of the house in which he lives on Earth—this one, though, has an eerie, green glow. In the mountains above, he makes out the giant shapes of ancient gods—Kali, Set—and a hideous beast that moves "with a curious lope, going almost upright, after the manner of a man. It was quite unclothed, and had a remarkable luminous appearance. Yet it was the face that attracted and frightened me the most. It was the face of a swine."

This creepy vision turns out to be prophetic. Soon the novel tells the strange tale of a battle between the diarist and a horde of these pig-men, of smaller size but of fleshier and more horrific presence than the vision. Hodgson ingeniously weaves together the horror of Circe turning Odysseus's men into pigs, the biblical overtones of demon-possessed swine, and the pig-human hybrids of H. G. Wells's *Island of Dr. Moreau*. Indeed, the prose begins to resemble something out of Wells, as a science-minded explorer tries to discern the line between the unnatural and the supernatural. The narrator's experiments are exaggeratedly methodical, which of course makes us skeptical of him. When the horde vanishes without a trace, his sister seems afraid of *him* and makes no mention of the pig-men. Later, he measures a subterranean pit in the cellars of the house by placing candles around its perimeter: "Although they showed me nothing that I wanted to see; yet the contrast they afforded to the heavy darkness, pleased me, curiously. It was as though fifteen tiny stars shone through the subterranean night." His efforts to map space seem futile or, rather, aesthetic. There's a tinge of the sublime horror of weird architecture and eldritch space to all of this. In effect, this metaphor, which likens the abyssal candelabra to stars, converts an obsession with space into an obsession with time.

The narrator is reading ("curiously enough") the Bible when he has another vision. It begins with a sound: "A faint and distant, whirring buzz, that grew rapidly into a far, muffled screaming. It reminded me, in a queer, gigantic way, of the noise that a clock makes, when the catch is released, and it is allowed to run down." But the clock in the study is in fact speeding up, the minute hand "moving 'round the dial, faster than an ordinary second-hand," the hour hand moving "quickly from space to space." The narrator looks out the window. What follows—a kind of ekphrasis of time-lapse film—is astonishing. While *The Time Machine* (1895) also describes time sped up, to my mind, Hodgson's language and imagery far surpass Wells's.

Surrounded by the "blur" of "world-noise," the narrator watches the sun go from orb to arc to streak to flicker to quiver of light. He sees clouds "scampering" and "whisking" across the sky; the "stealthy, writhing creep of the shadows of the wind-stirred trees"; and when winter comes, "a sweat of snow" that abruptly comes and goes, "as though an invisible giant 'flitted' a white sheet off and on the earth." He sees "a heavy, everlasting rolling, a vast, seamless sky of grey clouds—a cloud-sky that would have seemed motionless, through all the length of an ordinary earth-day." He grows used to "the vision of the swiftly leaping sun, and nights that came and went like shadows." The advancing edge of a black thundercloud flaps "like a monstrous black cloth in the heaven, twirling and undulating rapidly." He catches "glimpses of a ghostly track of fire that swayed thin and darkly towards the sun-stream . . . it was the scarcely visible moon-stream." Poor Pepper turns to dust. His own face has grown old in the looking glass. Eventually, he sees a long, rounded shape under the "aeon-carpet of sleeping dust" in the room—his corpse. It has been "years—and years." He has become "a bodiless thing."

At this point, the novel gets even weirder, merging spiritual and scientific language into a grand, universal theory of ghosts, angels, demons, heaven, hell, as well as planetary orbits and star deaths. Our ghostly narrator repeatedly hints that he has reached the end of time—yet time presses on. He drifts, without will, into unknown dimensions via large bubbles with human faces locked within them. Eventually, he watches as his house on the borderland—the borderland between what and what exactly?—is overrun with pig-men, set aflame as the Earth flies into the sun, and then rises again in the phosphorescent incarnation of the house from his first vision. He is borne toward it, steps inside, and wakes in his study. All is well, it was just a dream . . . except that poor Pepper is still a heap of dust.

The House on the Borderland closes with the vengeance and the patness of genre fiction. Pig-men, of a sort, return. The narrator gets another dog, who is also sacrificed to plot. H. P. Lovecraft (of all people) noted a touch of sentimentality to the novel, too. But I have never read a more remarkable account of time beyond a human scale. This account feels especially worth revisiting now, when time poses a new problem for humans: we're running out of it. Or it's running out of us—we are the grains of sand falling through the thin neck of years left before we reach three degrees too far.

How can we conceive of the time of climate change, the time of planetary death? *The House on the Borderland* tried to conceive of exactly this a century ago. Yes, the narrator's acts are fruitless. He gets haplessly carted about the universe to witness the end of time, which never really ends, is always at the edge, nearing an asymptote, on the borderland. Sure, his diary breaks off midspeech and Hodgson slams the frame story shut with an unsatisfying clunk. Still, I urge you to dwell in *The House on the Borderland*, to explore both its means—its ragged form and otherworldly atmosphere—and its ends: the sublimity and humility of recognizing just how uneasily we sit within the endless spinning of time.

LOLLY
WILLOWES
OR THE LOVING HUNTSMAN
SYLVIA TOWNSEND
WARNER

Chapter Nine

LOLLY WILLOWES

SYLVIA TOWNSEND WARNER

IVAN KREILKAMP

THE YEAR 1936 was a watershed for Bloomsbury fellow traveler Sylvia Townsend Warner. She traded a respectable existence editing *Tudor Church Music* for what Sarah Waters describes as "a kind of rural outlawry" in Dorset with the poet Valentine Ackland. The pair soon decamped for Barcelona as newly committed communists, to work with the Red Cross during the Spanish Civil War. And 1936 marks the publication of Warner's fourth novel, *Summer Will Show*, a passionate lesbian love story charged with political and sexual upheaval.

Sophia Willoughby, *Summer*'s wealthy Victorian heroine, travels to Paris in 1848 with the intention of reclaiming her husband from his French Jewish mistress, Minna. Instead, Sophia finds herself drawn to Minna "with a steadfast compulsive heat," "a thing not of the brain but in the blood" (120). Sophia trades English "cold-hearted respectability, . . . hypocrisy, . . . and domesticity" (179) for life with her husband's ex-lover in a bohemian Parisian underworld and eventually finds herself loading guns on the barricades.

A decade earlier, however, Warner's first novel, *Lolly Willowes; or, The Loving Huntsman*, told a more surprising and original tale about the journey from domesticity to wildness. In *Summer Will Show*, Sophia Willoughby's erotic liberation is enabled, and to a degree explained, by historical tumult in distant France. *Lolly Willowes* instead finds its heart of darkness in a placid modern-day English village, one that just happens to be a hotbed of demonic possession. Warner chronicles a self-effacing English spinster's gradual realization that, far from being a forgotten superfluity in the modern marriage market, she is actually a witch in league with Satan. It is as if Virginia Woolf had rewritten Nathaniel Hawthorne's story "Young Goodman Brown," complete with afternoon teas and a feckless nephew at Oxford.

Lolly Willowes initially presents itself as a conventional post-WWI spinster story. Its opening sentences find Laura (nicknamed "Lolly" by a niece) moving in with her elder brother, Henry, and his family after the death of their father, for whom she had cared for nearly a decade. "They took for granted that she should be absorbed into the household of one brother or the other. And Laura, feeling rather as if she were a piece of property forgotten in the will, was ready to be disposed of as they should think best."

Laura chafes inside a patriarchal English world defined by the mechanisms of ritual and tradition, but what can she do? She finds her sole means of escape in moments of vivid imagination. "She was subject to a peculiar kind of day-dreaming, so vivid as to be almost a hallucination: that she was in the country, at dusk, and alone, and strangely at peace. . . . Her mind was groping after something that eluded her experience, a something that was shadowy and menacing, and yet in some way congenial."

Only after Laura suddenly strikes off on her own, moving from her brother's home, in London, to a small village in the Chiltern Hills called Great Mop, does the novel's muted occult strain come to the fore. A small kitten turns up in Laura's rented bedroom. She is not sure how it found its way in, and when she reaches down to stroke it, it suddenly bites and claws at her, raising a single "bright round drop of blood." Laura is overcome:

> Not for a moment did she doubt. But so deadly, so complete was the certainty that it seemed to paralyze her powers of understanding, like a snake-bite in the brain. . . .
>
> She, Laura Willowes, in England, in the year 1922, had entered into a compact with the Devil. The compact was made, and affirmed, and sealed with the round red seal of her blood.

Satan had always had his eye on Laura, she now realizes: "The ruling power of her life had assaulted her with dreams and intimations, calling her imagination out from the warm safe room to wander in darkened fields." With the drop of blood raised by the mysterious kitten, Laura realizes that her straitened spinster experience had always been troubled by a barely discernible undertow. *Lolly Willowes* now morphs into a delightful novel of self-actualization through witchcraft. It beats *The Bloody Chamber* (Angela Carter's 1979 feminist reap-propriation of fairy tales) to the punch by half a century—and with a far lighter touch.

Great Mop soon turns out to be full of witches and war-locks, and in a pastoral Black Sabbath Laura enjoys a dance with a "pasty-faced and anaemic young slattern whom she had seen dawdling around the village . . . they whirled faster and faster, fused together like two suns that whirl and blaze in a single destruction. . . . The contact made her tingle from head to foot." This full-body tingling is the novel's only real hint of what *Summer Will Show* unfolds into explicitly lesbian eros. Witchcraft is neither lesbianism nor communism—at least, never explicitly so. Laura's taboo longing operates here instead as a deliciously subterranean force; we feel her desire all the more for its encoded disguise.

Laura's new identity as "the inheritrix of aged magic" releases her from those conventional mechanisms—of custom, tradition, duty—that had constrained her. In a long speech to Satan at the novel's conclusion, she offers a sweeping vision of an England filled with women whose birthright occult powers have been suppressed:

> When I think of witches, I seem to see all over England, all over Europe, women living and growing old, as common as blackberries, and as unregarded. . . . And all the time being thrust down into dullness when the one thing all women hate is to be thought dull. . . .
>
> Is it true that you can poke the fire with a stick of dyna-mite in perfect safety? . . . Anyhow, even if isn't true of

dynamite, it's true of women. Even if other people still find them quite safe and usual, . . . they know in their hearts how dangerous, how incalculable, how extraordinary they are. Even if they never do anything with their witchcraft, it's there—ready!

The brilliance of this novel lies in Warner's success in imbuing the "common," the ordinary, and even the "dull" with the force of dangerous magic while still permitting each to remain its ordinary self. Quiet English everyday realism is revealed as witchcraft—and as *having always been that way*.

Warner went on to write six more novels, along with a raft of other work, including poetry, short stories, and the first English translation of Proust's *Contre Sainte-Beuve*. Late in her life—in the stories of delightfully perverse fairy lore mostly published in the *New Yorker* and collected in the 1977 *Kingdoms of Elfin*—she turned to thoroughgoing fantasy. But never more successfully than in this first novel did she call out the imagination to wander—perhaps because in *Lolly Willowes* fantasy is so convincingly embedded in the everyday.

When first invited to be "absorbed into" her brother's household, Laura had "accepted the inevitable," and "behaved very well." However, the novel's turn to witchcraft (is it an early turn to magical realism as well?) rejects the inevitable and misbehaves, offering a beguiling vision of a world of incalculable women bearing within them disruptive dark powers. If *Summer May Show* trades English respectability for un-English bohemian revolution, *Lolly Willowes* pulls off the more difficult feat of making English respectability seem dangerously revolutionary.

Chapter Ten

MYTHOLOGY

EDITH HAMILTON

KATHRYN LOFTON

GROWING UP, my family had a patron: an artist who gave us his used Dodge Dart when my mom's job took her off a bus line and who sometimes handed me five-dollar bills at the end of his visits to our house. He was a deeply kind person who saw in our Erskine Caldwell clan something worth salvaging from the fate otherwise predicted by demographics.

When I was ten, he handed me a paperback copy of Edith Hamilton's *Mythology: Timeless Tales of Gods and Heroes* (1942) and said, "All educated people know mythology." I took the book and ran upstairs, where I immediately wrote my name and the date in ballpoint pen on the inside cover, as if the ink was an incantatory potion that would launch me to the ranks of the educated.

The scene sticks with me, I think, because so many of my earliest memories involve women teaching me to read and men assigning me things to read. As with most U.S. children who attend public schools, the majority of my instructors were female. As with most U.S. children, my mother was more involved in my educational development than my father. Social scientists work to get dads more involved because research indicates that fathers' involvement in their child's early education is correlated not only with academic success but also with improved overall well-being.[1]

Somehow, the absent figure is the most affecting, a myth unto himself.

In the weeks, months, and years after the slender book became mine, I read and reread the stories of love and adventure that Hamilton rendered so wryly: Cupid and Psyche, Pyramus and Thisbe, Orpheus and Eurydice, Pygmalion and Galatea. The stories had no Disney endings. They concluded with limited lover visitation or a harassed gal being turned into a linden tree.

I also drank in the Steele Savage illustrations (a 1970 reviewer in *The Classical Outlook*: "The illustrations are strikingly beautiful, although they bear a closer relationship to *Fantasia* than to anything Greek"). Was it weird to wish I could turn into a forever-bubbling spring (like Arethusa) or a shining-leaved tree (like Daphne)? I liked how overpowering emotions guided every mythological action and reaction: cockeyed desires strung together risk and longing, manipulation and capture. Part of the thrill was not knowing what role I wanted for myself in the story. "He decided that he could never rest satisfied unless he proved to himself beyond all doubt that she loved him along and would not yield to any other lover." That's Hamilton writing about Cephalus, but the line fits at least seven other characters. I wanted to be the one who stirred that desire, that impulse to possess. Or did I want to be the one who felt it?

The key plot point in these stories seemed to be pursuit. But it was pursuit inside a cloud unknowing, a shroud of darkness. A god chased you; someone accidentally stabbed you; you couldn't help returning to a spot where a first tryst occurred; you were visited for nighttime pleasure by someone you couldn't see. All of this stalking and constraint and strength of feeling made me feel a little woozy as I read in my bunk bed. I couldn't name what that wooziness was. I could only see myself wanting to recreate its conditions, over and over.

Much later, I'd focus my educated self on getting down and geeky on all of this. I'd learn about the role of women in Greek and Roman antiquity; how ancient Greeks and Romans perceived rape and how Athenian law adjudicated rape accusations; why Greeks liked to talk about love coming through arrows; how to conceive of consent in classical Athens; and how to teach rape scenes from Ovid's *Metamorphoses* in the era of trigger warnings.[2]

I would join a field—the study of religion—in which explaining the local mindset of seemingly awful things is standard practice. For example, one of the field's leading lights once explained (and later, upon reflection, modified) that the Greek goddess Persephone's "proper name" is "only bestowed when she has been initiated, become an adult, and lost her maiden status." What the original claim underlines is that the myth of Persephone should not be understood through modern ideas of rape. What we think about sexual violence today is unhelpful to understand the properly "cosmic event" recorded in the myth of Persephone.[3]

Hamilton, too, comments that being so initiated gains its subject "geographical fame," suggesting that Europa cut a deal for a spot in the atlas. "Nothing humanly beautiful is really terrifying," she writes, setting a stage for readers like me to think that when Zeus transformed himself into a bull and "lay down before her feet and seemed to show her his broad back," we should see the overwhelming power of beauty—not the overpowering power of power.

Hamilton isn't worried about power because she doesn't see Greek mythology as an articulation of a religious system that ordered real people's lives: "Greek mythology is largely made up of stories about gods and goddesses, but it must not be read as a kind of Greek Bible," she writes. "According to the most modern idea, a real myth has nothing to do with religion." These were stories, not manuals for right living. "For the most part the immortal gods were of little use to human beings and often they were quite the reverse of useful."

The professional person I have become is tempted to get lost in the debate about whether Hamilton has the distinction between myth and religion right. Perhaps this distinction is a practice of myth making. Stories can and do serve as manuals; religion, like myth, is not absolutely sequestered from scholarship.

Still, I can't stop thinking about how I got here. Thinking about all the men who handed me myths hoping to make me their educated equal, about the person I was, gobbling up every scrap they gave me. I remember how it felt so good, so sexy, when I could identify the figures in that Rubens painting or when I knew the W. B. Yeats allusion to Leda without looking it up.

Hamilton made the route to being clever very easy. It's hard to tell how much pleasure she extracted in her own life from this work. She was the kind of person who, according to her closest student, friend, biographer, and life partner, Doris Fielding Reid, "liked men better than women."[4] By her own description, she was a schoolmarm who taught generations of students at Bryn Mawr School, developing its rigorous classical curriculum and fundraising for disadvantaged daughters to gain access to elite education. Yet her legacy includes focusing on how to close your eyes and slide onto Mount Olympus via the back of a bull.

It was only long after I was handed *Mythology* that I would wonder if being understood as properly educated required the eminently useful myth that rape could be a cosmic event. It was still much later when I wondered: maybe it was an initiatory rite I needed to undergo in order to get my name into the atlas?

"The fact that the lover was a god and could not be resisted was, as many stories show, not accepted as an excuse," Hamilton explained in her version of Creüsa and Ion. "A girl ran every risk of being killed if she confessed." These are stories, we are told. I like to think she told them to us not to bring us to woozy oblivion. I like to think she hoped we might use our educated power to draw new maps.

NOTES

1. Alia Wong, "The U.S. Teaching Population Is Getting Bigger, and More Female," *The Atlantic* (10 February 2019); Anna Sarkadi et al., "Fathers' Involvement and Children's Developmental Outcomes: A Systematic Review of Longitudinal Studies," *Acta Paediatrica* 97, no. 2 (February 2008): 153–58.

2. Eva Cantarella, *Pandora's Daughters: The Role and Status of Women in Greek and Roman Antiquity* (Baltimore, MD: John Hopkins University Press, 1986); Karen F. Pierce and Sysan Deacy, eds., *Rape in Antiquity: Sexual Violence in the Greek and Roman Worlds* (London: Bloomsbury, 2002); C. Carey, "Rape and Adultery in Athenian Law," *Classical Quarterly* 45, no. 2 (1995): 407–17; Cristóbal Pagán Cánovas, "The Genesis of the Arrows of Love: Diachronic Conceptual Integration in Greek Mythology," *American Journal of Philology* 132, no. 4 (2011): 553–79; Rosanna Omitowoju, *Rape and the Politics of Consent in Classical Athens* (Cambridge: Cambridge Classical Studies, 2002); Elizabeth Gloyn, "Reading Rape in Ovid's *Metamorphoses*: A Test-Case Lesson," *Classical World* 106, no. 4 (Summer 2013): 676–81.

3. Bruce Lincoln, "The Rape of Persephone: A Greek Scenario of Women's Initiation," *Harvard Theological Review* 72, no. 3/4 (1979): 223–35; Bruce Lincoln, *Emerging From the Chrysalis: Rituals of Women's Initiation* (New York: Oxford University Press, 1991).

4. Doris Fielding Reid, *Edith Hamilton: An Intimate Portrait* (New York: Norton, 1967); John White, "The Hamilton Way," *Georgia Review* 24, no. 2 (Summer 1970): 132–57.

Chapter Eleven

OTHER LEOPARDS

DENIS WILLIAMS

EMILY HYDE

DENIS WILLIAMS was a painter in London, a novelist in the Sudan, an art historian in Nigeria, and an archeologist in his native Guyana: the polymath's polymath. He moved in and out of disciplines, institutional contexts, and metropolitan and anticolonial politics in the era of decolonization. Perhaps this restlessness explains his relative obscurity in any one field. His 1963 novel *Other Leopards* appeals precisely because it is disordered and contrarian—full of a thoroughly timely postcolonial ambivalence about disciplinarity, historiography, and possibly even history itself.

How best to sum up the hardwired recalcitrance of the novel's protagonist and narrator? Perhaps by saying that he'd likely be delighted by the daft list of descriptive metadata that JSTOR currently associates with this novel: "Topics: Verandas, Hell, Pumps, Ambivalence, Prime ministers, Cigarettes, Lamps, Knees, Pipe smoking, African culture." This preposterous list

appears (courtesy of JSTOR) at the head of an excerpt originally published in the November 1963 issue of *Transition*, one
of the premier political and cultural journals of anglophone
Africa in this era. As excerpted, *Other Leopards* may seem a
good match for *Transition*, striking a political note of postindependence disillusionment. It opens with a prime minister's
rousing speech in Jokhara (a lightly fictionalized Sudan) then
goes on to describe political strife between the Arab Muslim
north and the Black Christian south, as well as a strike by
latrine workers that leads to a coup d'état. "End of the private
joke of democracy, first try; no crying; no regrets," remarks
our narrator.

But *Other Leopards* is also a novel about art and culture. The
narrator is a West Indian archeological draftsman working at a
dig site near Meroë, an ancient city on the Nile. He has come
to Africa on a quest for "this ineffable what's-it, this identity,"
but he remains ambivalent about his African roots, Caribbean
upbringing, and European education. He's stuck in a hell of
his own making: his friends call him "the Uncommitted African" (there's more than a little Frantz Fanon here, not to mention Jean-Paul Sartre). He has two lovers: Kate, a white woman
from Wales, and Eve, an Afro-Guyanese woman also living in
Jokhara. He is equally vicious to both of them. What of *verandas*, *knees*, and *pumps*? Denis Williams the painter fills this
novel with visual detail, color, shadows, edges, and spaces. He
associates his lovers with landscapes: Kate with the "granite
hillsides and ruins and legends and history" of Wales; Eve
with the "dark silent creek-water" of Guyana and his "nameless
yearning for origins." (In short, the narrator's contrarian charm

occasionally tips over into trite and time-honored sexist stereotyping.)

JSTOR's metadata manages, though, to capture the text's more skittish tendencies, including the narrator's nervous, staccato sentence construction; the overused semicolon; his psychic distress. At the level of syntax and style, *Other Leopards* refuses logical, grammatical connections of cause and effect, before and after; the prose often reads as the incarnation of what grammarians call parataxis. The desert, for example, blinks suddenly into view: "No shade much, thorns; branches withered. Acacia scrub; life irreducible."

The narrator's style flouts the orderly connections that undergird the smug colonial teleology of history writing. It also, though, registers his psychological disintegration, which is inextricable from his disciplinary training in art history and archeology. Our narrator excels at reproduction, congratulating himself on being able to "draw the modeling on a grain of sand 1:3 scale." His employer is Hughie King, an Englishman who wants to put the ancient inhabitants of their dig site at Meroë "decently into history," which would mean proving that they were Black. But Hughie wouldn't presume to do this work himself—he sees it as his West Indian draftsman's responsibility to his history and people. "Hughie's Burden," the narrator sneers, "Hughie . . . forcing me on to some tour de force of art-scholarship in which I'd single out the wheat from the chaff in Meroitic Art and demonstrate once and for all (better than and long before Ifé) the ancient creativity of this Negro kingdom, *ergo*, of my race." The narrator rejects this burden and the art-historical scholarship it would entail. If the other option is forcing order upon history, he unhesitatingly prefers the madness represented by the novel's jittery stream-of-consciousness style.

Ironically, *Other Leopards*' hostility toward history gives it its literary-historical significance. It was written on the cusp between the exhilaration of independence (Sudan in 1956, Nigeria in 1960, and a raft of other Commonwealth nations soon thereafter) and the grim reality of power in the postcolony. It's a search for identity—a West Indian returning to Africa—but set in the wake of the joyous Négritude movement of Aimé Césaire and Léopold Senghor. While the Barbadian poet Kamau Brathwaite had spent half a decade in Ghana by 1963, *Other Leopards* appeared well before he developed his celebrated concept of "nation language." And the Trinidadian novelist V. S. Naipaul hadn't yet displayed his signature bullying scorn of Africa in *In a Free State* (1971) or *A Bend in the River* (1979).

Williams was born in British Guiana, won a British Council art scholarship to study in London in 1946, and thrived as a painter in London for about a decade: in the early 1950s he shared studio space with Francis Bacon, was cheered on by Wyndham Lewis, and placed work in *This Is Tomorrow* (1956), the watershed exhibition for the nascent British pop art movement. But in 1957 he left London behind for a job teaching in the Department of Fine and Applied Art at the Khartoum Technical Institute in the newly independent Sudan. Indeed, he worked as an archeological draftsman on a European-led dig at Meroë.

Other Leopards asks, in essence, if the postcolonial subject's identity can be formed in opposition to the disciplines and their colonial histories or if it must instead be formed by entering, even acquiescing to, those disciplines. At a crux point in the novel, the narrator encounters an image of Amanishakheto, queen of the kingdom of Kush from 10 BCE–1 CE. She is portrayed in relief on a pylon in the desert, flogging a group of slaves. In her millennia-old image, the narrator sees himself and all the other Afro-Caribbean characters in the novel, forever displaced by the legacy of the slave trade. He names her "The Queen of Time" but also identifies her with his lover Eve, making her a figure both of power and of sexualized violence. The narrator sees her as Black, but that vision collapses the colonial discourse that orders and historicizes art into history. The narrator decides to abandon "Hughie's Burden" because he cannot organize Amanishakheto's power, the European slave trade, and his own present in time.

This novel is not about an identification with the past as a basis for future development; it is a repudiation of historical time. Amanishakheto incarnates violence—she is a slave driver, in fact. Although the narrator's identity has been shaped by colonial histories he'd like to be able to discard, the Queen of Time is neither an origin point nor a solution to the dilemma of his Afro-Caribbean identity. After all, it is slavery—in Africa and in the Caribbean—that shaped the narrator and the world he fled, only to arrive in front of this image.

Denis Williams suffered no such paralysis. From the Sudan he moved to Nigeria, taking up teaching positions, studying classical West African art forms, and publishing in the fields of art history and archeology. He wrote only one more novel. Unlike many other West Indian writers of his generation, he returned to an independent Guyana in 1967, believing that a national identity could be built only on a multiethnic, multiracial foundation that incorporated Guyana's prehistory as well as its colonial-era history. He died in 1998, and Williams's daughters, Charlotte Williams and Evelyn A. Williams, have since paved the way for scholarly study of his painting, writing, art-historical, and archeological work. (In 2002, Charlotte Williams also published *Sugar and Slate*, a remarkable memoir about growing up estranged from her father in a small town on the coast of north Wales.)

Other Leopards is not just a novel from the era of decolonization; it's a novel about how hard it is to decolonize a discipline like history or art history. How do you undo systems of knowledge and representation that have shaped not just your education but your identity? The novel's unbalanced narrator offers no practical solution, but he does act out Fanon's claim—made in 1963, the same year *Other Leopards* was published—that "decolonization, which sets out to change the order of the world, is clearly an agenda for total disorder." The Queen of Time summons and then collapses nearly every ordering opposition in the book—African and European; Arab and Black; Muslim and Christian; slave and free; word and image; ancient and modern; then and now. But not male and female—that one remains, even in a novel so opposed to essentialism that it treats "Verandas, Hell, Pumps, Ambivalence, Prime ministers and Knees" as equally apt objects for its jumpy, unhinged gaze.

Chapter Twelve

SOLARIS

STANISLAW LEM

KATE MARSHALL

IS THERE a more entrancing account of an encounter with non-human sentience than Stanislaw Lem's *Solaris*? The reputation of this 1961 magnum opus of Polish science fiction, translated from the 1964 French translation into English in 1970, largely depends on various film adaptations, including Tarkovsky's stunning 1972 reimagining. Yet what keeps drawing me back to the original novel is something that eludes adaptation: the trenchant exteriority of the novel's ultimate protagonist, Solaris. Today, we have begun to grapple, tentatively, with the almost pantheistic notion that Earth's seas may be alive with a will and logic all their own. Lem's vision of oceanic vitalism likely speaks more cogently to readers today than it did to his audience half a century ago.

Solaris begins with the arrival of Kelvin, a scientist—an expert in "Solaristics," no less. He joins the bedraggled group of fellow Solarists on a space station orbiting the only planet of a binary solar system. The planet's entire surface is covered by one vast sentient ocean: think of that wave-wracked water world that greeted Matthew McConaughey in *Interstellar*. Kelvin finds himself in a decayed environment inhabited by elusive, unstable (and in some cases dead) colleagues. Even the scientist's landing on the station strikes a discordant note: rather than a human voice answering his hail, he hears "successive bursts of static . . . against a background of deep, low-pitched murmuring." It's as if "the very voice of the planet itself" were coming over his radio.

It is a bit tricky to relate Kelvin's mind-bending encounters with the vast being that covers Solaris without spoilers. One crucial point is that the ocean's strange properties relate to the planet's unlikely capacity to stay in a relatively stable orbit movement between its two suns: in other words, this particular three-body problem gets solved by intentional tidal forces. Perhaps as a corollary of its capacity to remain attuned to its environment in this way, the Solaris ocean reveals an uncanny capacity to mine the unconscious of its visitors, producing too-real reproductions of the lovers, children, or guilty passions that haunt them. Watching Kelvin interact with a vast intelligence that both shapes and reacts to his thoughts, readers come to ponder what sorts of immense hidden armatures may be sustaining and conditioning all they think and do.

Kelvin and the few remaining Solarists respond to the ocean's sentience by turning it into the protagonist of a fiction they weave around their close encounter. "Certainly it was only too obvious that the ocean had 'noticed' us," Kelvin says. "That fact alone invalidated that category of Solarist theories which claimed that the ocean was an 'introverted world,' a 'hermit entity,' . . . unaware of the existence of external object and events, the prisoner of a gigantic vortex of mental currents created and confined in the depths of this monster revolving between two suns." Instead, he asserts in a moment of clarity, "the ocean lived, thought, and acted."

Kelvin and company struggle to make sense of a planet-scale entity endowed with cognitive and intentional powers, to grasp its alienness without reducing it: "Like it or not, men must pay attention to this neighbor, light years away . . . a neighbor situated inside our sphere of expansion, and more disquieting than all the rest of the universe." He devotes himself to lessons in becoming a viewpoint, rather than a human observer. And like Lem's memorable comic creation, the space traveler Ijon Tichy (and like Tichy's direct descendant, Arthur Dent, in Douglas Adams's *Hitchhiker's Guide to the Galaxy*), Kelvin is well aware of the "temptations of a latent anthropomorphism."

It is respect for the Solaris ocean in all its ungraspable alienness that both tortures and inspires Kelvin. He reaches for a "long-distance view" of the ocean, then reverses the perspective, trying to see himself as "from a long way off, as through the wrong end of a telescope." This move, learned from looking at Solaris from ever-increasing intervals of distance, allows him the cognitive and narrative ability to grow smaller in relation to his environment. In Kelvin, Lem marries a very formalist sense of defamiliarization with the techniques of estrangement beloved in science fiction to create a flawed but compelling observer.

Jonathan Culler entitled a 1985 piece on Lem "If the Sea Were Intelligent," gesturing to an insight of Lem's that has even greater salience today, thanks to the cosmic implications of one aspect of global warming. Any aliens who happen to be observing Earth acutely enough will notice its orbit slowing down, and slowing down even more quickly as time goes on. If their scientists are shrewd, they may even discover that the agency behind this slowdown is a liquid one: the melting ice caps and their resultant contribution to global sea levels are changing the movement of the planet through space. The way that the water moves, masses, and incites a wobble in Earth's seemingly stable rotation may invite those aliens' attention and speculation.

It is as if the seas were able to rise up in response to our incomplete and feeble attempts to narrate the all-too-human causes of ocean change on a planetary scale. This science-fictional opportunity for an ocean to seize narrative control gives readers a better chance to imagine the elusive nonhuman world. *Solaris* offers up one of the twentieth century's great ecological protagonists, an entity that, in all of its impenetrability, presents an admittedly warped reflection of our own cognitive situation. Yet that very warp, that strangeness, may provide the best possibility of thinking about the outside that is always beside, always inside us.

Chapter Thirteen

RIDDLEY WALKER

RUSSELL HOBAN

PAUL SAINT-AMOUR

GROWING UP, I knew and loved a string of books written by Russell and illustrated by Lillian Hoban. My sister and I read them—*The Mole Family's Christmas, The Sorely Trying Day, The Stone Doll of Sister Brute*—to tatters, often quarreling over who got to go first. Somewhere in our copy of the Hobans' *A Bargain for Frances* the sentence "Paul is stuped" is furiously graffitied in Renée's handwriting.

Years later, I came across a 1980 experimental novel called *Riddley Walker,* a postapocalyptic bildungsroman set three millennia after a nuclear war has leveled the earth's cities, irradiated the environment, and decimated the living. Surely the author couldn't be *that* Russell Hoban, the one who wrote the egg song in *Bread and Jam for Frances?*

Poached eggs on toast, why do you shiver
With such a funny little quiver?

None other. That it sprang from the same pen as the Frances books, though, is far from the most remarkable thing about *Riddley Walker*, whose New Iron Age characters huddle in small fenced settlements near Canterbury, surviving by hunting and farming and salvaging metal from the remains of their ancestors' self-immolation. Literacy being both rare and restricted in this England, the larval government communicates through propagandistic puppet shows that are interpreted by each settlement's "connexion man." Riddley, twelve when the story begins, is one such connexion man, just come of age.

Four decades on, the book's unique language—fans call it "Riddleyspeak"—is what separates Hoban's novel from the rising tide of dystopian coming-of-age books. The Kent shown on the map that heads *Riddley Walker* (figure 13.1) is not our Kent. Canterbury has become "Cambry," Ashford is "Bernt Arse," Dover is now "Do It Over." And the English that greets us on the first page of text is not our English.

> On my naming day when I come 12 I gone front spear and kilt a wyld boar he parbly ben the las wyld pig on the Bundel Downs any how there hadnt ben none for a long time befor him nor I aint looking to see none agen. He dint make the groun shake nor nothing like that when he come on to my spear he wernt all that big plus he lookit poorly. He done the reqwyrt he ternt and stood and clattert his teef and made his rush and there we wer then.

This looks at first as if the narrator were speaking aloud in an extreme regional vernacular. But it turns out that Riddley is *writing* his story. And as the novel's postapocalyptic premise comes into focus, we learn that its language grows straight out of that premise. Hoban has imagined how English might look and work after a near-total social collapse and 3,000 years of linguistic drift.

As a reader of James Joyce's most contortionist writing, I approached Riddleyspeak knowing a good pun or portmanteau word when I saw one. I appreciated how a feeling of *releaf* carried with it a vision of the blasted world regreening; how to *breave* poisoned air was also to experience bereavement with each brief breath; how keeping a *red cord* instead of a record made writing both a rubric and an umbilicus.

But *Finnegans Wake* works by floating thousands of unrepeated neologisms past its reader. Hoban's book asks you instead to learn a lexically stable if imaginary dialect of English. And hanging over that language acquisition is a haunting historical question: What has happened, in the millennia that separate Riddley from his readers, to produce this language and the worldview it encodes?

That question intensifies around the corroded words from late twentieth-century science and technology that appear in Riddley's narrative. Here, *blip* means true, to *pirntowt* is to reckon, to *progam* is to plan, and when you test a theory you *spare the mending*. Riddley and his people dimly sense that "chemistery and fizzics" might help them get "that shyning Power back from time back way back . . . what had boats in the air and picters on the wind."

The vocabulary of atomic physics, though, has been composted together with bits of Christian theology, pre-Christian

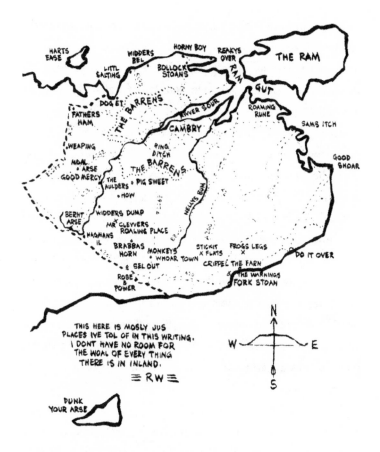

belief, postdisaster invention, and the life of Saint Eustace. The result is not twentieth-century science revived but a new faith, one that darkly prophecies the rediscovery of "the 1 Big 1," when "the Littl Shynin Man the Addom" is pulled in two.

History is not bunk in *Riddley Walker*, but it is a winding stair. We can never set the *red cord* straight, any more than Riddley can, about what made his world and his language what they are. Midway through the novel, another character presents our hero with a surviving fragment of late twentieth-century prose and proceeds—hilariously, grotesquely—to misinterpret it. Just as we're feeling fluent in Riddleyspeak, the novel hands us back our own standard English as a nearly unintelligible artifact.

This gut punch makes us wonder how well we've really understood the book's alien dialect, whose meaning rests on the radical misrecognition of a lost past—one that happens to contain us. Sure enough, the novel has a word for this reading in the dark: *terpitation*. Yes, the echo of "turpitude" reminds us that interpretation is a fallen state, one in which our only method is trying to "plot the parbeltys" by "tryl narrer." It's a fallen state we share, however, with the book's characters. These are among the most feverish exegetes in fiction, deciphering and re-deciphering everything from puppet shows to children's rhymes as if the future depended on it. At times, they seem as uncertain of the meaning of their own world as we are of their words.

That shared uncertainty is a kind of glue for Hoban's fan community, which every year on his birthday (February 4) posts quotations from his work in public places on sheets of his beloved yellow A4 paper. Literary feast days can be monumentalizing—think Bloomsday—but this one feels fugitive, dimly lit, distinctly Riddleyesque. To come upon a few lines of Hoban taped to a bench or stapled to a telephone pole is to receive an anonymous invitation: come puzzle with us. Come and terpit.

Riddley Walker is now a touchstone for novelists who invent strange dialects for the inhabitants of stranger worlds to speak.

David Mitchell has acknowledged the debt owed to Hoban by his novel *Cloud Atlas* (2004), whose far-future middle section is set in a postcollapse Hawaii and narrated by one Zachry Bailey in a Pacific variant of Riddleyspeak. Will Self's *The Book of Dave* (2006) is unthinkable without *Riddley Walker*, to which Self penned a loving introduction in 2002. Paul Kingsnorth's *The Wake* (2014), whose narrator recounts the Norman invasion in an adapted "shadow" version of Old English, was linked to Hoban's book in its UK jacket copy and in every second review.

It is a mistake, though, to overstate the resemblance between Hoban's book and Kingsnorth's. *The Wake*'s nostalgia for a pre-Conquest England (and English) aligns all too well with Kingsnorth's pro-Brexit stance and his claim that high levels of immigration into the UK have forced real Brits to ask, "What does it mean to be 'us' in England?" Hoban, who was born in Pennsylvania to Ukrainian Jewish immigrant parents and spent half his life as an expat in England, had no such impulses. Far from rolling English back to some imaginary pure state, *Riddley Walker* is a heaving stew of loan words, linguistic drift, and cultural shift.

The novel is a preemptive strike against bids, like Kingsnorth's, to make the world safe again for English nativism. It is in this that *Riddley Walker* most spills out of its Cold War context. The novel's Kent could have been a hothouse for xenophobic localism. But the nuclear war that kicks off the Bad Time is a worldwide disaster with planetary sequelae. The altered coastline of Riddley's map drowns marshes and makes islands of hills and bluffs, implying that global sea levels have risen some twenty feet. And a key ingredient in the novel's chemistery and fizzics plot comes from across the English Channel, hinting that the novel's "Inland" is about to be reinserted into broader itineraries of exchange, conflict, and "Plomercy." Hoban's Kent doesn't epitomize the local; it metonymizes the world.

Riddley Walker deserves its cult status for making us feel spectral in the midst of life: it confronts us with a posterity that looks back at us as blankly as we peer at it. But I keep rereading—and on the slenderest pretext teaching—Hoban's book as much for the smaller discoveries. Like the best of the Hobans' children's books, *Riddley* can turn a word from a stone you kick on the road into a thing that kicks back. It bids you "[put] your groan up foot where your chyld foot run nor dint know nothing what wer coming," condensing all of that knowledge-to-come in the word *groan*.

"Paul is stuped," wrote my sister. I see now that she had invented her own Riddleyspeak, a writing whose very errors struck home. *Stuped*: that's me—wrong-footed, slouching, a biped stunned and bent. *Stil*, as Hoban's protagonist says, *I wunt have no other track.*

PART III

COMEDY

JOHN GAY'S *The Beggar's Opera* asks its readers to decide: "Should [art] be savage, grim, driven by white-hot rage? Or should it be smiling, gracious, and indulgent?" Yoon Sun Lee's answer is *both*—and that dichotomy applies in different ways to each of these books, jolly or satirical. To Lee, John Gay's "lasting accomplishment is to operate on two levels at once: to illuminate vividly the corrupt world while celebrating the capacity of music to find sweetness beyond it." Maud Ellman finds the metamorphosis at the heart of David Garnett's *Lady Into Fox* both absurd (does that fox actually *enjoy* listening to someone reading Richardson aloud?) and profound: "Wild we begin toward one another—at day's end, wild we remain."

Sean McCann admits that Mary McCarthy's "pen was a scalpel, her eye a coolly dispassionate instrument for dissecting the charades of the *bien-pensant* and self-regarding." Nonetheless, he finds in "Rogue's Gallery" a revealingly warmhearted and "sly rewriting of *The Great Gatsby*." Comparing Charles Portis's *Gringos* to a Crown Vic (look it up on the internet, young friends), Carlo Rotella worships the way "his prose can carry, with no apparent effort, such a charge of complex feeling—at once funny and sad, mock epic and genuinely stirring." Stephen McCauley, a celebrated comic novelist, turns to Christopher Isherwood (rather than the unapproachable Nabokov) when he thinks about crafting characters. Isherwood may claim "I am a camera," but in truth, "the reader is always aware of him manipulating the camera, outside the frame but ever present."

Chapter Fourteen

THE BEGGAR'S OPERA

JOHN GAY

YOON SUN LEE

IN AN age of seamless, brazen, total corruption, how should art be? Should it be savage, grim, driven by white-hot rage? Or should it be smiling, gracious, and indulgent? If your answer is "all of the above," *The Beggar's Opera* is for you.

Performed more often than any other play in the eighteenth century, John Gay's 1728 work was a game changer. By penning fresh lyrics to sixty-nine wonderful songs—well-known ballads, folk songs, arias, and dance tunes—Gay invented (or at the very least popularized and canonized) the *ballad opera*. On the surface, his characters' actions and language satirize contemporary social and political corruption. But woven throughout is music that uncovers tenderness, humor, and melancholy as well as rage; these songs both enhance and transcend the play's essential bitterness.

The curtain rises on a respectable businessman reviewing his "large book of accounts." Peachum is a thief-taker (an actual eighteenth-century institution) who employs criminals, profits from their thefts, and turns his employees in for a reward to be hanged when their productivity declines. The thief-taker is virtually indistinguishable from his best friend, Lockit the jailkeeper. Both were understood by contemporary audiences as allusions to the prime minister, Robert Walpole, the master and font of all corruption. Like a lawyer—Peachum compares himself to one in his opening song—each of these figures "acts in a double capacity, both against rogues and for 'em," invoking the law when it suits him, ignoring it when convenient, and raking in fees and bribes either way.

This is a world in which money does anything and goes anywhere and the law is merely an instrument for those with capital and without scruples. It serves the powerful and harasses the poor. Everything is subordinate to the form of the business model, including marriage, love, family, and friendship. As he betrays his own son-in-law, Peachum cheerfully points the moral: "Every man in his business. So that there is no malice in the case."

Against such figures of the law, the opera sets the highwayman Macheath: handsome, irresistible, an instant cultural icon ("Oh the shark has pretty teeth, dear . . . "). Onstage and off-, all the women are in love with him; all his fellow thieves admire him. He is the most universally valued, the most valuable, and thus the most vulnerable in terms of the plot. He can be turned in by anyone who's been his lover, rival, or accomplice—that is to say, the entire world. So of course it happens. Sitting in the condemned cell in the final act, Macheath sings broken snatches of folk songs and ballads in a parody of Italian opera's recitatives: "O cruel, cruel, cruel case! Must I suffer this disgrace?"

The scene suddenly veers away from pathos, though, when Macheath breaks into Gay's most memorable, magnificently angry song, set to the tune of the beloved ballad *Greensleeves*:

> Since laws were made for every degree
> To curb vice in others as well as me,
> I wonder we han't better company,
> Upon Tyburn Tree!
> But gold from law can take out the sting,
> And if rich men like us were to swing,
> 'Twould thin the land, such numbers to string
> Upon Tyburn Tree!

Gay brilliantly turns a ballad about unrequited love into a lyrical howl of rage at the systemic inequality of justice's application. Lady Greensleeves becomes Tyburn Tree, the gallows imagined as the object of an elusive fantasy in which not poor but rich criminals hang—every last one of them.

In the end, though, Macheath gets his reprieve. The opera's author, the beggar of the title, wanders onto the stage to concede that "an opera must end happily." "In this kind of drama, 'tis no matter how absurdly things are brought about," he notes. So it ends with mirth, joy, and a dance for everyone, including the "rabble."

Gay's opera offered its audiences the pleasure of recognizing afresh what they already knew: not only the tunes but also the "moral" that the beggar says he had hoped to convey through Macheath's execution: "that the lower sort of people have their vices . . . as well as the rich: *and that they are punished for them.*" The arbitrary happy ending doesn't uphold that last bitter punch line, but the world outside the theater did and still does. Money alone deserves love because it equals—and equalizes and absolves—everything. In this inescapably "rational" world, there are only the brute contradictions of society: the rich who get richer and the poor who get poorer.

That mixture of sardonic surface and lyrical undertow makes *The Beggar's Opera* a gift that keeps giving through the centuries. Exactly two hundred years after *The Beggar's Opera* premiered, Bertolt Brecht and Kurt Weill spun it into *The Threepenny Opera*, using the same characters, names, and relationships. The world of the original *Beggar's Opera* was already ruled by the calculation of profit and loss and the exchange of money: "Money well timed, and properly applied, will do any thing," as one character cheerfully remarks. The plot only needed a little updating to suit a more advanced stage of capitalism, in Weimar Germany, with references to banks, boards, and military imperial ventures.

It will be intriguing to see what the 2028 reinvention will look like—and inconceivable to imagine one not taking place. As long as capitalism endures, the social, political, and economic conditions for a new *Beggar's Opera* are always with us. Its lasting accomplishment is to operate on two levels at once: to illuminate vividly the corrupt world while celebrating the capacity of music to find sweetness beyond it. "Through the reconciliation that its formal law brings to contradictions, [it emphasizes] the real lack of reconciliation all the more. . . . As something that has escaped from reality and is nevertheless permeated with it, art vibrates between this seriousness and lightheartedness." Theodor Adorno's words describe the achievement of John Gay's clear-eyed, disenchanted, cruel, and merry opera.

Chapter Fifteen

LADY INTO FOX

DAVID GARNETT

MAUD ELLMANN

THE PUBLICATION of David Garnett's first novel, *Lady Into Fox*, shot the author into literary stardom, winning both the Hawthornden Prize and the James Tate Black Prize for Fiction. Despite his success in his own day, however, Garnett the writer (son of Constance Garnett, storied translator of Tolstoy and Dostoyevsky) has receded from view. If it weren't for his colorful sex life among the "Blooms Berries"—as Katherine Mansfield dubbed the influential modernists at the time—his prolific writings might have been forgotten. Much talked about as the lover of the artist Duncan Grant and later as the middle-aged cradle snatcher of Grant's daughter, Angelica Bell, "Bunny" Garnett nibbled more than his fair share of Blooms Berries while also browsing on exotic fruit from other gardens.

Published by Chatto & Windus in 1922, the traditional annus mirabilis of modernism, *Lady Into Fox* has received little attention from scholars of the movement. This neglect is partly owing to the story's genre: Kafka's *The Metamorphosis* (1915) aside, fable and fantasy tend to be marginalized in modernist studies. Fable is also associated with children's literature, and the first edition of *Lady Into Fox* could have been mistaken for a children's book. Barely ninety pages long, it was illustrated with charming woodcuts by the author's first wife, Ray Garnett.

Despite its juvenile appeal, however, *Lady Into Fox* is a very grown-up story drawn from multiple literary sources. As a tale of animal metamorphosis, the novella harks back to Ovid, as well as to a global treasure trove of folktales about animal brides. Even there Garnett belongs only obliquely. Barbara Fass Leavy's *In Search of the Swan Maiden* shows that in folktales many species—not just swans but also cats, foxes, frogs, moose, pigs, and seals—are married by choice or by force to men. Sometimes these brides are restored to their original human form as a reward for their domestication; in other cases, they revert to wildness. In Garnett's fable, though, the wife turns into a fox, rather than the fox into a wife.

In 1879, Richard Tebrick marries Silvia Fox without suspecting that his modest country bride might take after her name. The metamorphosis occurs when the couple is strolling in the woods: *"Where his wife had been the moment before was a small fox, of a very bright red."* Barely doubting that this vixen is indeed his wife, Mr. Tebrick sneaks her back into their home.

From then on the Victorian husband has to learn to share a house with a wife who grows foxier by the hour, despite her ludicrous efforts to remain a lady. Encouraging these efforts, Mr. Tebrick dresses her in feminine garb and feeds her grapes—on Aesopian authority—to erase the stench of fox.

Nonetheless, while reading Samuel Richardson's *Clarissa* aloud to his wife, Mr. Tebrick realizes that her attention has pivoted toward a caged dove rustling nearby; her reversion to nature seems inevitable. Dismayed by her behavior, Mr. Tebrick takes to drink, spending the night in such "beastly" depravity that the narrator primly draws a veil over the details.

In this marital contest, both spouses seem to be striving to convert each other to their mode of being, as if they were confusing kin with kind. Mr. Tebrick tries to change his wife back into a woman while Mrs. Tebrick tries to drag him down— quite literally—to her own level. She succeeds in coaxing him onto "all fours" during his drinking binge; presumably, she also lures him into bestiality, although this inference is left to the prurient reader. When she finally flees into the forest, it is her husband who goes animal, turning into "a touzled and disheveled figure" who rejects his own species much as Gulliver repudiates his fellow Yahoos after his encounter with the Houyhnhnms. Lovesick for his animal bride, Mr. Tebrick never regrets the disappearance of his human wife: "No, all that he grieved for now was his departed vixen."

Eventually Mr. Tebrick rediscovers his vixen in the woods, where she proudly presents him with her litter of five cubs. Although jealous of their dog-fox sire, her husband persuades himself that his honor cannot be "sullied by a beast" and that his wife "does right to be happy according to the laws of her being." Thereafter he comes to love her family, christening her cubs and giving his favorite the name Angelica. He even promises to pay for their education. This idyll comes to a violent end when a pack of foxhounds catches scent of Silvia, who springs into her husband's arms just before the dogs close in for the kill. Both Tebricks are "terribly mauled," but the husband survives the attack, whereas the vixen dies in his embrace.

Garnett's modernist contemporaries were enraptured by the story. "At last, at last, the Hawthornden has chosen the right book," Virginia Woolf enthused. Joseph Conrad declared, "The whole psychology of man and beast is, I should say, flawless, in essence and exposition." Even H. G. Wells chimed into this chorus of acclaim: "It is as astonishing . . . [as] a new sort of animal . . . suddenly running about in the world. It is like a small, queer furry animal, I admit, but as alive, as whimsically inevitable as a very healthy kitten. It shows up most other stories as the clockwork beasts they are."

The novel's popularity transcended the battle of the "brows," appealing to those with both high and low tastes. Its catchy title generated many spin-offs, both in fiction (including Christopher L. Ward's playful parody *Gentleman Into Goose*) and in advertising (the National Fur Company adopted the tagline "Lady Into Mink" in 1935). As late as 1962, the French writer Vercors (a.k.a. Jean Bruller), author of the most famous novel of the French Resistance, *Le silence de la mer* (1942), inverted Garnett's fable in his novel *Sylva*, where a fox turns into a woman. A ballet version of *Lady Into Fox* opened in London in May 1939, and several movie versions have been proposed, though none produced. The last bid was made by an Australian filmmaker who hoped to shoot the film with a cast of real foxes, but despite months of training, like Silvia Fox, they preferred to stay wild.

Critics today remain wary of Garnett's fable, suspicious of its implicit sexism. Gay Wachman describes *Lady Into Fox* as a "whimsically misogynist fantasy." In a similar vein, John Lucas in his study *The Radical Twenties* interprets Garnett's novel as a reaction against women's growing power in the public sphere: "*Lady Into Fox* implies that the real prison cage is the feral nature in which women are trapped and from which they perhaps can't be freed, no matter how solicitous their menfolk happen to be." This reading, in my view, underestimates the novel's foxiness. For one thing, Lucas assumes that the story takes the husband's side, whereas Mr. Tebrick is presented as a stuffed shirt whose solicitude would be tyrannical if it weren't so fatuous. Even his sanity is put into question: the local gossips think he has gone mad because his wife has run off with a lover, reducing him to a shaggy and deluded misanthrope.

In the tradition of animal fables going back to Aesop, *Lady Into Fox* invites allegorical interpretation—but also destabilizes any one-to-one correspondence between symbol and meaning. For this reason the story lends itself to contradictory interpretations. On the one hand, Mrs. Tebrick could be seen as a protofeminist who escapes her oppressive marriage to take a dog-fox as a lover, only to be hounded to death by the forces of convention. Alternatively, she could be seen as a New Woman whose animal lust imperils the foundations of civilized society. An early reviewer observed: "Like life itself this little story is continually suggesting an allegory without being one."

Garnett himself insisted that critics who search for hidden meanings are wasting their time, "for the value of all works of art is their face-value and not a hidden value." Nonetheless he later contradicted this assertion, claiming that *Lady Into Fox* does contain a moral—or an antimoral: namely, the absurdity of the idea of marital fidelity. But this self-serving moral also misses the point. To my mind the story gestures to something darker than adultery, something more like Jacques Lacan's cryptic axiom: "There is no sexual relation."

What we behold in *Lady Into Fox* is the breakdown of a marriage brought about by the fundamental incompatibility between the sexes. Garnett's story intimates that the sexual relation rests on the delusion that kin can be converted into kind. If the fable also applies to same-sex love (and I think it does), then perhaps Garnett's point is darker still: every kind attempt we make to "claim kin" with one another is a sort of violence. Wild we begin toward one another—at day's end, wild we remain.

Chapter Sixteen

PRATER VIOLET

CHRISTOPHER ISHERWOOD

STEPHEN McCAULEY

JUDGING FROM his writing, Christopher Isherwood must have been an ideal guest at a dinner party: intelligent, witty, interested in and insightful about others without seeming judgmental. In some of his best books (*Goodbye to Berlin*, *Down There on a Visit*) his narrator is named "Christopher Isherwood," but you'd never accuse him of the self-absorption found in any number of best-selling memoirs or the multivolume autobiographical novels currently clogging bookstore shelves. When he finally wrote an actual memoir (*Christopher and His Kind*), he wrote it in the third person, as if he needed to make an other of himself to justify the self-examination. It seems likely Isherwood always made the person sitting next to him feel like the most interesting guest at the table, which is, after all, one definition of charm.

Sandwiched between some of Isherwood's better-known books and often overlooked is a slim 1945 novel called *Prater*

Violet, a minimasterpiece that's well worth hunting down, whether or not you're already a fan. The book contains much of Isherwood's understated elegance, his insight into behavior, and all of his powerful charm. As an added bonus, it's a literary novel about that decidedly unliterary global obsession: moviemaking.

It's 1933 and "Christopher Isherwood" is hired by a British studio to work with an Austrian director named Friedrich Bergmann—a fictionalized Berthold Viertel, a semisuccessful director with whom Isherwood worked in the 1930s. For Bergmann—Jewish and Austrian—the political situation in Europe is a lot more urgent than for most of the British characters in the novel. " 'Cousin Edith's dentist,' said my mother, as she passed me the teacup, 'seems to be quite convinced that Hitler's going to invade Austria soon.' " "Isherwood" criticizes her sources, but admits to being "in a very good humor" as he does so. After all, he's just been offered a job in "pictures"! The movie "Isherwood" and Bergmann are working on is called *Prater Violet*, a trifle replete with disguises, mistaken identities, and an implausibly happy ending. The triviality of the material is an ironic counterpoint to the dire political situation looming in Bergmann's home country.

As Bergmann and "Isherwood" collaborate on the screenplay, Bergmann coaxes dialogue out of "Isherwood" by acting out full scenes, inhabiting multiple characters, limning their psychologies, and laughing and weeping as they would. In the same mode, he acts out the proceedings of the Reichstag Fire Trial taking place in Berlin. "Isherwood," like his mother and brother, sits back enjoying the performance, detached from its content. It's a striking example of Isherwood's willingness to portray the naiveté of his fictionalized self as equal to that of everyone else.

Isherwood's flawless powers of description make the process of shooting the movie feel immediate, even when some of the techniques employed are primitive by today's standards: "The problem of camera noise is perpetual. To guard against it, the camera is muffled in a quilt, which makes it look like a pet poodle wearing its winter jacket." But there's nothing dated about the mix of flimsy illusion and artistic magic that defines the atmosphere of the set. On the one hand, "This is literally a half-world, a limbo of mirror-images, a town which has lost its third-dimension"; on the other, "Bergmann's concentration is marvelous in its singleness of purpose. It is the act of creation."

My love of Isherwood stems primarily from his ability to bring characters to life on the page, contradictions and all, with a few simple strokes. When I'm stuck in my own work, I often pull a volume of Isherwood off the shelf and open at random to a passage that describes a person with what I can convince myself is attainable brilliance. (Versus, let's say, the showy, utterly unobtainable genius of Nabokov.) Here's one such passage from *Prater Violet*: "Lawrence was the head cutter on our picture: a short, muscular, angry young man of about my own age, whose face wore a frown of permanent disgust. We had made friends, chiefly because he had read a story of mine in a magazine, and growled crossly that he liked it."

I especially love "growled crossly." It burns the irascibility of the character into your mind while illustrating "Isherwood's" eagerness to accept flattery, even when delivered with a cranky rumble.

As characters go, Bergmann is the triumph of the novel, an outsized presence physically and intellectually. His long diatribes on love, politics, and industry gossip anchor every scene, and the presence of this Austrian Jewish man in the midst of a largely detached British public is both a reproach to political indifference and a harbinger of things to come. Thanks to Isherwood's observational prowess, Bergmann remains plausibly human in his complexity: "The face was the face of an emperor, but the eyes were the dark mocking eyes of his slave—the slave who ironically obeyed, watched, humored and judged the master who could never understand him."

So verbose is Bergmann, so heavy his directorial hand, it's sometimes easy to forget "Isherwood" is an actual player in the production of the film and action of the novel. Isherwood practiced self-effacement over the course of his career. His most famous line, after all, is: "I am a camera . . . quite passive, recording, not thinking." Yet the reader is always aware of him manipulating the camera, outside the frame, but ever present.

In *Prater Violet*, the author steps into the frame in the splendid final pages. Bergmann and "Isherwood" are walking the streets after a wrap party for the film. "It was the hour of night when the street lamps seem to shine with an unnatural, remote brilliance, like planets on which there is no life." Bergmann is, for once, silent, and for the first time, we glimpse "Isherwood's" life. (Even the most "charming" dinner guest has to give something of himself lest he appear voyeuristic.) His homosexuality is unspecified but clearly indicated. His musings on his love life, death, and the oppressive power of fear serve, in the matter of a few pages, to connect the thematic dots of the novel. The yearning that has trembled under the surface of the book's comedy emerges powerfully, and what had been an entertaining novel suddenly becomes an unforgettable one.

Mr. Isherwood, the dinner invitation's in the mail.

Chapter Seventeen

"ROGUE'S GALLERY"

MARY McCARTHY

SEAN McCANN

ABOUT HER wit there was never disagreement. It was sharp, and it was cold. Even by her own account, Mary McCarthy's pen was a scalpel, her eye a coolly dispassionate instrument for dissecting the charades of the *bien-pensant* and self-regarding. Stalinist intellectuals, bullying husbands and adulterous lovers, craven politicians and manipulative artists. Everywhere she looked McCarthy saw self-deception and moral cowardice, greeting it (so she told her friend Hannah Arendt) with "bitter exaltation." In her best-known books—*Memories of a Catholic Girlhood*, *The Group*—and in her legendarily ruthless reviews and essays, McCarthy lanced the pretenses of the smug and lambasted the dishonesty of the powerful. Her admirers saw McCarthy as a wicked satirist. To her critics, she was simply heartless. No one ever called her a warm and fuzzy writer.

Yet there is "Rogue's Gallery." Where did it come from, this odd tale plopped into the middle of her first book,

The Company She Keeps? Even in that quirky, loosely arranged collection of stories McCarthy persisted in calling a novel, "Rogue's Gallery" is an awkward party crasher. The tale has little to say about Meg Sargent, the brash protagonist McCarthy modeled on herself. Also missing are the perennial concerns that made McCarthy a feared combatant in the macho literary circles of mid-twentieth-century New York. "Rogue's Gallery" has nothing to say about the moral evasion of left-wing literary intellectuals, the bad taste of middlebrow artists, or the self-regard of entitled men.

Instead, McCarthy's story zeroes in on a lovable conman whose escapades Meg recalls in the form of a memoir at first uproariously funny and then surprisingly sad. A one-time bootlegger turned small-time art world hustler, Mr. Sheer runs a failing antiques business (Meg is a sometime employee) and dreams of someday entering a world of wealth and status. In the meantime, he struggles to survive on two unreliable sources of income. When he is not convincing rich clients to invest in miniature crystal portraits of their beloved dogs, Mr. Sheer is borrowing and then fraudulently selling other dealers' merchandise: a *Better Call Saul* of the 1930s. Meg renders his whirling efforts to stay a half-step ahead of his creditors in a tone that can only be called loving.

What accounts for that affection? Curiously, Meg appears to be drawn to her dishonest boss precisely because he proves indifferent to the values she holds most dear. Meg thinks of herself as brutally honest. Mr. Sheer prefers an artful lie to the plain facts. For Meg, art is an Olympian pursuit of truth.

Mr. Sheer is certain beauty is a hustle and scholarship a sales pitch—the more rococo in its evasion of the facts, the better.

As she sweats out the summer months in Mr. Sheer's down-at-the-heels office, reading Proust and worrying about her moral integrity, Meg marvels at discovering a man entirely deaf to her most treasured concerns. He "could hardly tell a Cellini from a Remington," she observes. But Mr. Sheer worships "any kind of ingenuity: boxes with false bottoms, cuckoo clocks, oval miniatures of the school of Boucher that opened if you pressed a button and disclosed a pornographic scene." The more desperate his circumstances, the more earnestly does he keep his faith in guile and trickery and the hope that they will someday land him the respectable life he has always craved.

The sheer unlikelihood of that hope gives "Rogue's Gallery" its air of slapstick hilarity and, at first, appears to lend the story its pathos. Like many another tale of an endearing swindler, "Rogue's Gallery" is in essence the story of a naïf in a cruel world. Or, rather, two naïfs. Bouncing stoically back from every defeat and humiliation, Mr. Sheer takes on a kind of Chaplinesque dignity, if only because he remains blithely unaware of the clumsiness of his dreams.

"From his Western boyhood," McCarthy reports in appropriately deadpan style, Mr. Sheer "had loved dogs and culture." Meg Sargent, his chronicler and would-be protector, serves as his straight man. She struggles earnestly to keep him from harm's way and to lure him toward the paths of the law-abiding. But her efforts inevitably crumble before the chaos his schemes unleash. "We would take the cage into the inner office," Meg recalls of the canine models who bring Mr. Sheer his sole legitimate revenue, "open it, and the animal would shoot out and bite me on the leg."

Like all McCarthy's best writing, "Rogue's Gallery" draws heavily from personal experience. In the summer of 1932, when she was between her junior and senior years at Vassar and pursuing a courtship with Harold Johnsrud, the actor who a year later would become her first husband, McCarthy found a temporary job working as a secretary for Manny Rousuck, a midtown gallerist who specialized in "sporting" art of hounds and hunting scenes. It wasn't long before McCarthy discovered Rousuck's business was pure facade. He had no goods, few clients, and little prospect of paying McCarthy's wages or avoiding eviction.

Yet McCarthy stayed on with Rousuck that summer, weathering with him the nadir of the Great Depression. She lent him the occasional price of an automat dinner, covered for him when his creditors came calling, and worried anxiously about his compulsive drive to deceive his customers and colleagues and his habit of bending the law. When she graduated from college (and again when her first marriage broke up a few years later) McCarthy returned to Rousuck's employ, calling on her high-class education to lend his sales pitches an air of refinement. Decades later, long after Rousuck had managed to become an unlikely success at the prestigious Wildenstein gallery, McCarthy would still rely on his friendship and his skill at turning up a car or an apartment or a stylish hat in a pinch. When Rousuck died in 1970, she mourned that she had lost one of the "pillars of my life."

It cannot have hurt McCarthy's appreciation for Rousuck that both her first husband and her second—the eminent critic Edmund Wilson—disliked the conman-cum-gallerist intensely. Wilson, who resembled his predecessor Johnsrud in being intellectually authoritative and cruelly domineering, complained that Rousuck appealed to McCarthy's "outlaw side." If so, Mr. Sheer represents a fear that must have haunted McCarthy as she pursued her own outsize ambitions.

In the design of McCarthy's book, Mr. Sheer is a foil to Meg Sargent. Yearning, as McCarthy did, for eminence and professional autonomy, Meg hopes that she can gain esteem on the strength of her talent and integrity. Every step of her path, though, runs through a dishonest and predatory society. Like Mr. Sheer, Meg is a lonely striver, struggling bravely to stay afloat in a harsh world and compelled against her own better inclinations to make recourse to a little stagecraft now and then. Along with Mr. Sheer she cannot ignore a fact the comfortable pretend to forget—that life is nine-tenths pretense and posture. That awareness makes Meg, like McCarthy, a gimlet-eyed satirist. If it turns Sheer into a fabulist and huckster, Meg comes to believe it is also what makes him a romantic lover of beauty.

As in most romances, Mr. Sheer's quest must fail. Like Meg, the reader knows that sooner or later the charm will wear off, the lies and half-truths no longer convince. Yet Mr. Sheer's love of fraud and his talent for mishap do not lead to quite the disaster we have been led to expect: they bring him wealth and respectability instead. Once the worst years of the Depression have passed, Mr. Sheer is surprised to learn that his talents are in fact just what the luxury trades need. The big-name gallerists come calling and explain that in his quest to sell "bric-a-brac to rich dog and horse people," Mr. Sheer "had been a pioneer." He is soon launched on a disappointingly legitimate career, no longer a vendor of frauds and fancies, but a salesman of objets d'arts to the tasteless rich. The transition breaks his heart, just as it saddens Meg. "Mr. Hyde," she laments, "had turned into Dr. Jekyll."

In this way, "Rogue's Gallery" turns out to be McCarthy's sly rewriting of *The Great Gatsby*. Like Fitzgerald's protagonist, Mr. Sheer is a poor boy from the Midwest who yearns to rub shoulders with the American aristocracy. Like Gatsby, he doesn't much mind if that quest demands some extralegal machination or a bit of imposture. In McCarthy's world, however, there is no Tom Buchanan against whose hard malice Mr. Sheer's dreams might crack up. The sad truth is that the engines of American capitalism love a scam and are eager to give it a patina of respectability.

In the years that followed *The Company She Keeps*, McCarthy would go on to achieve the esteem she had always sought. But she would never lose the sense that her keen intelligence was a gift to be preserved from a sea of comforting falsehoods and patronizing men. "Rogue's Gallery" reminds us that, earnestly though she longed for status and success, McCarthy could not help loathing respectability or, even against her own better judgment, loving an artful masquerade. Her pen dissected the self-deception of the contented. Her affections remained with the outlaw.

Chapter Eighteen

GRINGOS

CHARLES PORTIS

CARLO ROTELLA

FAITHFUL READERS of Charles Portis tend to be rabidly in love with his writing but a little mystified by its potency. Like a retired Crown Vic Interceptor acquired at a police auction, its souped-up engine and superhero frame masked by quotidian dings and a relaxed feel in the joints, Portis has a deceptively conversational plain style that turns out to be plenty powerful beneath the hood. An Arkansan who served in the marines during the Korean War and worked as a newspaper reporter in New York and London before returning home to write novels, Portis is perhaps best known for the film adaptations of his only best-seller, *True Grit*, and for declining to participate in promoting himself or his writing. Over the years, though, a coterie of hardcore admirers has singled him out as a craftsman of great virtuosity and originality.

Hoping to figure out at long last how his prose can carry, with no apparent effort, such a charge of complex feeling—at once funny and sad, mock epic and genuinely stirring—I find myself rereading his five novels in a perpetual cycle: *Norwood* (1966), *True Grit* (1968; John Wayne starred in a film adaptation in 1969, and the Coen brothers' version came out in 2010), *The Dog of the South* (1979), *Masters of Atlantis* (1985), and *Gringos* (1991), his secret masterpiece.

Gringos is a deceptively taut and moving novel about an American in Mexico, Jimmy Burns, who used to traffic in looted pre-Columbian artifacts. It begins:

> Christmas again in Yucatán. Another year gone by and I was still scratching around this limestone peninsula. I woke at eight, late for me, wondering where I might find something to eat. Once again there had been no scramble among the hostesses of Mérida to see who could get me for Christmas dinner. Would the Astro Café be open? The Cocina Económica? The Express? I couldn't remember from one holiday to the next about these things. A wasp, I saw, was building a nest under my window sill. It was a gray blossom on a stem. Go off for a few days and nature starts creeping back into your little clearing.

Though I have read that opening paragraph dozens of times, the way the former tomb raider's unhurried musing on local dining options leads to a bolt of insight into the entropic temporariness of civilization still gets me every time. Revelation turns out to have been sneaking up on both narrator and reader from the start, its dire grandiosity interwoven with easygoing self-deprecation, a trademark Portis effect.

Evangelizing readers of Portis tend to come up with elevator-pitch analogies on the order of *He's like Mark Twain meets Cormac McCarthy!* I will grant that if McCarthy had a sense of humor and Twain had lived long enough to write about sticky clutches and post-hippie drifters, together they might have come up with Jimmy's comment on blasting an antagonist in the face at close range with two shotgun barrels of No. 2 goose shot: "I wasn't used to seeing my will so little resisted, having been in sales for so long." But such comparisons can do only partial justice to Portis.

Casting about for ways to account for the effect of his words on the page, I asked some eminent and accomplished Portisians to explain what they found so compelling about his writing. Roy Blount Jr., a master of humor that relies on voice rather than punch lines, once wrote, "The only adequate response to a Charles Portis novel is to jump in the air, do a flip, and wind up on your feet, like Cheetah the chimp in the Tarzan movies when intensely pleased."[1] Blount's e-mail exchange with me centered on the narrow but crucial angle of distinction between Portis's characters and narrating voice. "Not only do the characters take themselves seriously, but so does the author take them," he wrote. "So how can they be so funny? There must be some other consciousness behind the author. Maybe the reader is looking over the author's shoulder as he looks . . . No, that can't be it. Worth considering: Portis told me how much he loved Borges."

Ian Frazier—a veteran contributor to the *New Yorker* and the author of a dozen acclaimed books, ranging from *Coyote vs. Acme* to *Travels in Siberia*—pointed to Portis's mastery of bathos, particularly his characters' ability to sustain high-minded intent amid humiliating conditions, as well as his expert deployment of naive narrators whose lack of a sense of humor is itself hilarious. But Frazier located the wellspring of Portis's power not in technique but in theme. "What looks like style in Portis's writing is actually substance of the most profound kind," he wrote to me. "Portis is different because he is coming from deeper in the American experience, and from a time America has forgotten about. The country used to be about the Protestant faith working itself out in a new country." Noting that "the plots of Portis's books tend to be about the progress of various pilgrims," he cited an exchange in *True Grit* between fourteen-year-old Mattie Ross and the horse trader Colonel Stonehill, who describes the obstacles Mattie faces in her planned pursuit of her father's murderer into Indian territory. Mattie replies, "The good Christian does not shrink from difficulties."

Taken together, Blount's and Frazier's comments make sense of one of Portis's signature traits. Instead of cataloguing their sorrows or plumbing the mysteries of their faith, his characters tend to dwell upon the details of car repair or the excessive prices of needful items, indulging an eagerness to explain how things work as a way of masking their reluctance to discuss the most deeply felt aspects of their own inner lives.

Here's Jimmy Burns, late in *Gringos*, swearing off once and for all his career as a looter of antiquities, during an encounter with a former business associate: "I said I probably wouldn't be venturing out much anymore, into the *selva*. He opened the car door, and a pomegranate rolled out. Neither of us made a move to pick it up. A sour and messy fruit. Somebody gives you one and you haul it around until it turns black or rolls away out of your life." Five sentences so simple that they muster only two commas among them, and half the passage is a digression on the mechanics of the pomegranate, yet somehow it manages to convey a final renunciation and possible rebirth. Or take the sentence that opens the second chapter. In twenty-two words, Jimmy manages to sum himself up as a capable guy who has never managed to amount to much and lacks a sustaining sense of purpose: "You put things off and then one morning you wake up and say—today I will change the oil in my truck."

When you champion a writer whom you regard as underappreciated, it's never clear to what extent you're trying to get others to appreciate your writer and to what extent you're trying to show how much more discerning you are than everyone else. Perhaps it's really your own greatness, not your beloved writer's, that you consider underappreciated.

In other words, as Blount and the novelist Ed Park have pointed out, passion for Portis can turn you into a Portis character.[2] His books are full of sects, secret societies, enthusiasts animated by a self-regarding rage for the obscure. The wildly unreliable Dr. Reo Symes in *The Dog of the South*, who has a habit of picking his nose and scraping the leavings onto the pages of whatever he's reading, believes that all other writing collapses into "foul grunting" when compared to *With Wings as Eagles*, a self-help book written by a salesman-drifter named John Selmer Dix. "Dix puts William Shakespeare in the shithouse," Symes declares.

I just barely resist the temptation to say something similar about Portis. That police-auction Crown Vic may not look like much, but when you step on the gas you feel as if it could achieve escape velocity.

NOTES

1. Roy Blount Jr., "Charles Portis," *Arkansas Life* (December 2010), 18.
2. Ed Park, "Like Cormac McCarthy, but Funny," *The Believer*, no. 1 (March 2003), https://believermag.com/like-cormac-mccarthy-but -funny/.

PART IV

BATTLE AND STRIFE

WAR IS not only hell; it's also a hell of a mess. Beware books that draw bright clear lines across its muddy fields—conversely, look out for the ones that manage to bring its awful untidiness onto the page. Lauren Kaminsky and Steve Biel feel the presence of the Great War in Mary Borden's experiments with anonymity, interchangeability, and the powers of distance: "from the lacerated ground, airplanes look like dots in the sky, while soldiers and civilians are similarly microscopic glimpsed from the air." Upmanyu Pablo Mukherjee finds the same scalar shifts in Alexei Tolstoy's magisterial *The Road to Calvary*. The novel reminds him—a century on from the Russian Civil War it documents—that "living when all that is solid is melting into air takes practice." Jonathan Bolton praises Czech novelist Ivan Olbracht for spinning a tale about "a magic green bough that deflected bullets as a farmer on a July day might shoo the swarming bees." Ultimately, however, Olbracht's triumph is "depicting messy conflicts with many sharp edges, and characters who are confused, riven by conflicting emotions even as they are raked across the grain of state power."

Closer to our own day, Steve Biel, writing solo this time, praises Gustav Hasford's *Short-Timers*—the novel that inspired Kubrick's *Full Metal Jacket*—for not trying to evade "the most persistent source of anguish in war stories: the sense of a vast experiential and moral distance between the battlefield and the home front." That gap also looms large in Robert Stone's *A Flag for Sunrise*: "Break your heart, this book" is novelist Ben Fountain's final verdict on its tale of the unwinnable and indeed unwageable Third World shadow wars ignited by a bellicose imperial America. Isabel Hofmeyr, in a similar vein, dubs the Zimbabwean Dambudzo Marechera "the writer of the garbage dump," to whom all life is a dispersed, baffling battlefield stretching over the "wreckages of utopia" that pile up in the postcolony. In another key, Lorraine Daston praises Philip Fisher's erudite *The Vehement Passions* for the way it locates within our own intermittently controllable bodies the emotional impulses that send people out to die—whether out of the fury of their own emotions or by proxy, serving the mobilized wrath of others.

Chapter Nineteen

ROAD TO CALVARY

ALEXEI TOLSTOY

UPAMANYU PABLO MUKHERJEE

IF YOU are a Russian writer called Tolstoy, you forever lurk in the great shadow cast by your namesake. After all, what could compare to *War and Peace*? Now imagine a distant relative of Leo Tolstoy born during some of the most tumultuous decades in modern history to aristocratic parents with the requisite scandalous lives (adultery, duels, etc.); imagine him growing up as a radical antimonarchist interested in the classic writings of Marx and Turgenev (to whom he was also related, through his mother) but also the adventure tales of Victor Hugo, James Fenimore Cooper, and Jules Verne; caught up in the hurricane of the Russian Revolution and the devastating civil war that followed and casting his lot with the "White" forces against the Bolsheviks; going into a five-year exile in Paris and Berlin after the communist victory; choosing to *return* to the country now called the Soviet Union and becoming one of the most acclaimed authors of this new land; living through the devastations of the Second World War; and becoming a key investigator of the genocidal crimes committed by Hitler's regime. Finally, imagine this "Comrade Count" winning the Stalin Prize for an epic novel of his own in 1943.

Today, we are afflicted with both historical myopia and amnesia. The Russian Revolution is shrink-wrapped in clichés about Lenin, Stalin, and Trotsky. Historians sugarcoat or pass over in silence the subsequent invasion, starting in 1918, of Russia by the allied forces of Japan, Britain, the United States, Canada, Australia, Czechoslovakia, and others. Do we even consider, let alone reckon with, the sheer scale of the Russian Civil War's carnage—including an estimated 300,000 to 450,000 army casualties—and its subsequent effects on the Soviet Union?

Alexei Tolstoy's life was its own kind of epic. Between 1921 and 1940, though, he somehow produced a three-volume novel that brilliantly depicts the Russian Revolution not as a historic inevitability but as wildly contingent, a messy game of chance played by flawed humans with desires both noble and harmful. He realized that both the revolution and the subsequent civil war called not for another *War and Peace* but for a compelling experiment in genre busting. Yet who reads the three volumes and 500,000 words of *Road to Calvary* now? Throughout the Soviet Union and the socialist-bloc countries it sold millions in the 1940s and 1950s. Latter-day readers, however, presume the Great Dictator's prize axiomatically makes *Road to Calvary* just another propagandistic example of dreary "socialist realism"—centered on heroic factory workers and their battles to temper steel.

Pick up Edith Bone's lucid translation of the novel and you discover a world so large that representing it requires a dizzying array of formal devices. Consider the beginning of the first volume:

> Long ago, in the far-off days of Peter the Great, the verger of Holy Trinity—a church still standing near Holy Trinity Bridge—was coming down from the belfry in the twilight when he saw a banshee—a bareheaded, gaunt woman; he was very frightened and afterwards shouted at the inn: "A desert will be in the place of Petersburg" . . . One day eyewitnesses saw the devil himself riding in a droshky on Vassilov Island. Then again, one midnight, when a gale was blowing and the river was in spate, the bronze Emperor leaped from his granite rock and galloped over the pavement stones. On another occasion a Privy Councillor riding in his coach was accosted by a dead man—a dead government clerk who pressed his face to the coach window and would not let go.

We are closer here to Andrei Bely's bizarre modernist masterpiece *Petersburg* than an ode to Stakhanovite welders. And this weird, gothic, nightmarish world is never dismissed as an archaic relic of the past. Rather, it coexists with various others: the futurist one of "scientific" development, the apocalyptic one of total warfare, the claustrophobic and slyly oppressive one of the "respectable" people, the extravagantly decadent but ennui-laden one of the super-rich, the bleakly survivalist one of the peasants and the urban poor.

Most interesting of all, these coexisting worlds demand distinctly different composition styles. So urban gothic appears cheek by jowl with Zolaesque naturalism; satiric comedy of manners, with pastoral sentimentality; and, yes, socialist realism, with existentially absurd moments that recall Gogol and Dostoevsky. Admittedly, this experiment is not always successful. The plot is woven loosely round two couples: the sisters Daria and Katia and the friends Roschin and Telegin, who end up fighting for opposing armies in the civil war. Thanks to often-clunky coincidence, these pairs traverse the huge social scale of revolutionary Russia as they are repeatedly separated and reunited by the buffeting winds of history. Nor is the ratio between different generic registers perfect: do we really need hundreds of pages of regimental lists, battle orders, and tactical maneuvers at the virtually total expense of the comic, sentimental, or gothic?

These failures, though, are frequently redeemed by the writer's uncanny ability to give equal space to apparently incommensurable worldviews and perspectives. Peasants, sailors of the legendary Black Sea Fleet, a "White" general, rogue partisan leaders, bureaucrats and morally opportunist artists—each holds center stage and dictates the novel's narrative logic, at least briefly. This does not lead us to some kind of radical relativism where all these positions are held to be valid. Rather, the approach tries to present the vision of a singular but unequal and uneven world held together by its own tensions and contradictions—both material and ideological. Here is Sharygin, a young Communist League member, being quizzed by sailors of the Russian Black Sea Fleet to whom he had been preaching about the science of revolution a moment ago:

> "All right. Now answer me this question: without ability you can't even set a stove in the bath-house, without ability your wife can't even make the dough rise properly. So is ability wanted or isn't it?"
>
> Sharygin answered him: "See, comrades, what Latugin is driving at? Ability is something peculiar to the individual, and hence it is dangerous because it can lead a man to bourgeois anarchism, to individualism."
>
> "There you go." Latugin flapped his hand with a gesture of despair. "First chew up and swallow and digest these long words; then you can use them."
>
> The stoker angrily growled from his hatch: "Ability, eh? We know your sort! Nails dyed with sandalwood, bell-bottomed trousers, gold chain round the neck. . . . Ability indeed! . . . What you need is ten years sweating in the stokehold."

All fixed and settled notions about the "science" of revolution are unmoored. The people are full of prejudices, conflicts, hopes, illusions. Living when all that is solid is melting into air takes practice. In that practice people find a sense of belonging without ever erasing their differences. As a diagnosis of modernity, it is hard to improve upon.

Chapter Twenty

THE FORBIDDEN ZONE

MARY BORDEN

STEVEN BIEL AND LAUREN KAMINSKY

MARY BORDEN'S taut masterpiece has long been overshadowed by the other Great War books of 1928–1929 (*All Quiet on the Western Front, A Farewell to Arms, Good-bye to All That*) and by the 1922 war novels of Edith Wharton (*A Son at the Front*) and Willa Cather (*One of Ours*). To understand why, consider how the narrator of its opening sketch, "Belgium," calls the reader to attention: "You see those men, lolling in the doorways—uncouth, disheveled, dirty? They are soldiers. You can read on their heavy jowls, in their stupefied, patient, hopeless eyes, how boring it is to be a hero."

With the anonymity of "those men" *The Forbidden Zone* resists the comforts of identification with developed characters. To the generals who command them, these men are cannon fodder. Treating them any differently on the page would falsify frontline experience. *The Forbidden Zone's* relative neglect over the last nine decades signals something about readers' unwillingness to confront the private soldier's disposability.

Borden wrote most of *The Forbidden Zone* between 1914 and 1918, but she only published it after the immediate success of *All Quiet on the Western Front*, which she believed would "strip the glamour from modern warfare." Remarque's novel, though, does not convey the alienation and dehumanization of the world's first fully industrialized war as fully as *The Forbidden Zone* does. Borden's writing bears the formal imprint of mechanized violence and mass destruction that is the hallmark of war to this day. From the lacerated ground, airplanes look like dots in the sky while soldiers and civilians are similarly microscopic glimpsed from the air.

Divided into two parts, "The North" and "The Somme—Hospital Sketches," *The Forbidden Zone* contains seventeen pieces and no unified narrative. (The original publication included a short final section of poems, which recent editions have wisely omitted.) The first seven pieces are marked by dizzying shifts in perspective that, among other effects, mimic the experiences of two of the war's signature technologies: trenches and airplanes. We begin in the mud, where "there's no frontier, just a bleeding edge." A narrator explains that this is what is left of Belgium—"Come, I'll show you"—but the first-person disappears as quickly as it arrived. The second story, "Bombardment," opens at the break of day memorialized in trench poetry for the sublimity of nature and danger of battle renewed. In the stillness of dawn, "a speck appeared in the great immensity. It was an aeroplane." First seen from below, "superbly poised now in the spotless sky," the plane abruptly becomes the observer, as "a cluster of houses collapsed, while a roar burst from the wounded earth," sight arriving before sound. From above, the plane sees "signs of terror and bewilderment . . . in the human ant hill beneath it." But before we settle into the viewpoint of Borden's mechanical protagonist, the plane again becomes a "speck in the infinite sky, then nothing," as "the town was left in convulsions."

Even when the perspective shifts from sky to ground, no individual characters are distinguishable. "The Regiment" opens with clouds in a summer sky, "superb castles of white vapour, floating towards a land called No Man's Land," and with a passing airplane "bent on mysterious adventure." From an uncertain height, we glimpse a "moving mass of men" marching with "the steady jolting gait of weary animals." Suddenly, the narrator stands among them: "I saw in their eyes that they were men." Borden forecloses any move toward individuation by the men's arrival in a town square, where they are met by a group of officers and addressed by a general. Unlike the regiment, Borden's officers seemingly possess "variety": "No one was like another one. Not one had gestures like another one. Not one had clothes like another one. Certainly they were individuals." Yet these officers' individuality is merely asserted, not developed, and the story remains at the level of groups and types. A bugle heralds the arrival of what the regiment collectively sees as "a beautiful animal dressed as a nun and branded with a red cross" and the town collectively sees as a "white peacock": the first of many nurses in Borden's stories.

It is nurses, not soldiers, who bring a degree of intimacy to *The Forbidden Zone*. The first-person narrator of "Moonlight," awaiting her midnight shift, is lulled toward sleep by "the soft concussion of distant shells bursting from the mouths of cannon" but kept awake by the "little whimpering voice of a man who is going to die in an hour or two." The sounds and smells of war are naturalized by the inverted world of the field hospital. "I could sleep with the familiar damp smell of blood on my apron," she explains, "but the terrible scent of the new-mown hay disturbs me." A fever dream animating a rich psychic landscape, "Moonlight" is a relief to read after so many stories of distancing and alienation. Still, even in "Moonlight," and in the two stories that follow, each about a wounded soldier brought to the hospital to die, Borden's narrators could be any nurses anywhere along the Belgian front.

Not until the ninth story, "Enfant de Malheur," do readers learn some names: Pim the nurse and Guerin the priest. The protagonist stays nameless, though. "His name was tattooed on his arm," the narrator informs us in the story's opening line, but she doesn't reveal it. He is one of a group of Parisian convicts serving life sentences who have been drafted into the colonial army to fight in the trenches, and the story recounts his terror at the brink of death. He clings to his awareness of his "unutterable vileness" against Guerin's insistent prayers. When he finally offers his confession, "pouring out all his dark, secret, haunting memories into Guerin's ears and sobbing with relief," the narrator realizes that she will "never again in this world see anything so mysterious." Borden has finally invited us into the struggles of a distinctive character (still a type—"these assassins, thieves, pimps and traffickers in drugs" whose skulls, ears, foreheads, jaws, and mouths betray a genetic proclivity to criminality) whom the narrator explicitly seeks to preserve from the anonymity of mass death. "'No one, no one else must die tonight,' I kept saying to myself. 'There is only one death here tonight.'" Arrayed against this yearning for a unique, memorable death are the wooden crosses in the hospital cemetery marking the graves of past patients. "I could not remember them," the narrator grieves. "They had no names, no faces in my memory."

The Forbidden Zone's nurses express a combination of anguish and satisfaction that no doubt bears some relationship to the author's own war experiences. While she was pregnant with her third child, Borden signed up as a nurse with the London Committee of the French Red Cross. At the beginning of 1915, she set off for Belgium, leaving young children and an unhappy marriage to found her own field hospital on the road between Dunkirk and Ypres, a mere seven miles behind the firing line. The hospital's 5 percent mortality rate was the best of the entire front that year; according to her biographer, Jane Conway, wounded men pleaded to be sent there. After founding a second hospital on the Western Front in 1917, Borden became the first American woman to be awarded the Croix de Guerre. She dedicated her book "to the *poilus* who passed through our hands during the war," but she insisted it was "not meant for them." To these soldiers and the nurses who treated them, her writing, she confessed, could at best offer a "blurred" and "softened" version of the war's "bare horror."

Pained by the volume and pace of the mortally wounded becoming the forgotten dead, nurses in *The Forbidden Zone* experience an ecstatic sense of belonging—"bliss"—through shared suffering. In "Blind," when a young soldier crying for his mother dies with his head on a nurse's breast, she wonders if he thought "the arms holding him when he jerked back and died belonged to some woman I had never seen, some woman waiting somewhere for news of him in some village, somewhere in France." Recalling "those men" at the beginning of the book, "some woman" in the mind of an unnamed nurse imagining the dying thoughts of an anonymous soldier belies the scene's sentimental trappings. In hindsight, the narrator confesses that "because our mortality at the end of three months was only nineteen per cent, not thirty, well it was the most beautiful place in the world to me. . . . I think of it now. I only knew it then, and was happy. Yes, I was happy there." But this happiness is built on forgetting, and the experience of reading *The Forbidden Zone* mirrors that dissociation.

At the end of "Blind," after the maternal tableau, the narrator hears the cries of the eponymous blind soldier. He fears that she has forgotten him in the confusion of the ward—and she has—but she lies and assures him otherwise. When he smiles, she flees, sobbing. "I was awake now, and I seemed to be breaking to pieces." *The Forbidden Zone* is similarly fractured, and Borden refuses us the comfort of stitching the pieces together or holding on for long to any of the nurses and soldiers who populate its pages. The kind of warfare Borden documents is over a century old. Yet her experiments with anonymity and interchangeability—unlike more canonical modernist forays into interiority and individuation—make the Great War seem new and razor-sharp.

Chapter Twenty-One

NIKOLA THE OUTLAW

IVAN OLBRACHT

JONATHAN BOLTON

SOME OF Central Europe's greatest political novels have been meditations on disillusionment. Many of them—from Arthur Koestler's *Darkness at Noon* to Milan Kundera's *The Joke*—dramatize the inner journeys of intellectuals coming to terms with the flaws of communist ideology. *Nikola the Outlaw*, published in 1933 by the Czech novelist Ivan Olbracht, is different. Taking an illiterate bandit as his hero, Olbracht fashions an adventure tale that is equal parts political parable and romantic legend.

To be sure, Olbracht (1882–1952) excels at exorcising political fantasies. Early in the novel, for example, the peasants and poor Jews of the tiny village of Koločava rise up against their masters. They break into the home of a notary who has been cheating them and seize his safe, the symbol of a power they don't really fathom. They pound it and pound it but can't break it open, and they eventually abandon it in the snow, "with its paint scratched off and with hundreds of dents made by the woodmen's axes." When a new militia rides into town to restore order, its leader, Mendel Wolf, simply takes "a little key and open[s] the safe," removing a stash of documents the illiterate peasants would not have been able to read, as well as 300,000 crowns in cash, which conveniently disappear. The rebellion's leaders are dragged out of bed, beaten, doused in cold water, and led away in chains. The militia, now called a "national guard," loots the peasants' huts. "Things got back to normal," says the narrator, mimicking the voice of law and order: "Everything was as it should be."

There is something bracing about this story. As readers, we are being taught a healthy appreciation for the forces of political violence underlying language and ideology. From there, we may even be lulled into a smug sense of our own sophistication— this rebellion was never going anywhere, we tell ourselves. And yet *Nikola the Outlaw* never lets us settle into a comfortable cynicism about the distribution of power.

In the early 1930s, even Ivan Olbracht's fans would have been forgiven if they did not see a great novel in his future. He was a dedicated member of the Czechoslovak Communist Party through the 1920s and worked as an editor at the communist newspaper *Rudé právo*. Although he had published several novels in his twenties and thirties, including the forgettable *Anna Proletářka* (Anna the proletarian), he had devoted himself largely to political journalism and political agitation. In 1929, however, Olbracht was fired for protesting against the newly militant leadership of the party. At age forty-seven, he found himself expelled from the party and out of a job.

Looking for inspiration, he set off for Subcarpathian Rus', a remote and sparsely populated territory that had been awarded to Czechoslovakia in the peace settlements after World War I. There, in the easternmost part of the republic, he stumbled on the story that became his modernist magnum opus. A local lawyer told him of the robber Mykola Šuhaj, who had been hunted down a decade earlier after a two-year run of stealing from the rich and giving to the poor. Olbracht combed through courthouse records and then traveled to Koločava to interview Šuhaj's family. From his findings, he conjured up a political novel about a bandit with a magic green bough that deflected bullets "as a farmer on a July day might shoo the swarming bees." In a world where "everybody promises peace, but only when he shall have won," Nikola offers a rebellion of the spirit—one that won't dissipate like the peasants' futile uprisings.

At first, Nikola wants to stay out of trouble. When he deserts from the army, he acquires some local fame by eluding gendarmes for several months. But then he marries his beloved Eržika, hoping to settle down: "He had every expectation of having many children and not enough corn porridge, much want and a few transitory joys." One day, he comes upon some children playing in a meadow: one cracks a whip at his friends and shouts, "I'm Nikola Šuhaj!" In other words, they are playing at being *him*, waving the green bough he supposedly uses to swat away arrows and bullets.

In Olbracht's tale, myth precedes reality and calls it into being. Nikola falls into thought. He had, indeed, survived the world war. "Was there any kind of firearm that had not been used against him?" he asks himself. "Was there another man alive who could have evaded such a shower of bullets?" What if he really *did* have a green bough? "Nikola Šuhaj's pace grew slower. The soil was muddy and his steps soundless. To the left of him the brook murmured and rushed, rolling in turbid waves where there should have been waterfalls." Why should you live so wretchedly, the wilderness seems to whisper, when you hold an enchanted bough in your hand?

The rest of the novel plays out Nikola's rise and inevitable fall. Olbracht builds his story around a crucial insight: the Šuhaj legend had gained hold just as Czechoslovakia was taking over the administration of the territory of Subcarpathian Rus'. In a double-edged metaphor, Olbracht's narrator says that Šuhaj was to be the "touchstone" of state power: "There could be no order, and the authority of the new state could not be established, as long as this bandit was at large, as long as legends should be woven around his person." Nikola grows into the myth that has been forming about him, and we see each of his exploits get magnified in the telling and retelling, until he seems to be everywhere and nowhere. "A man in the woods was like a fish in the lake: everybody knew he was there but nobody knew just where."

Everyone is hunting Nikola, but the narrator's closest attention is devoted to the intersecting and conflicting interests of Koločava's inhabitants. Olbracht's narrative talent shines as he channels the thoughts of one group after another, exposing not just their self-deceptions but also the wishes and fears hidden beneath. There are the peasants, enigmatic and silent, whose every step is a transgression against the powers that be; the Czech gendarmes, war veterans sent off into a godforsaken backwater that grows more hostile and inscrutable by the day; and the town's Jewish elders, accustomed to negotiating with whoever is in power in order to preserve their community's (and their own) interests.

Olbracht, who was half-Jewish, would later set a second great work in Subcarpathian Rus', *The Sorrowful Eyes of Hannah Karajich*, portraying the plight of its impoverished Jews with imagination and sympathy. But his worldview was ultimately neither religious nor ethnic. It was political, and like a good communist, he zeroed in on money, class, and violence as the levers that move society. One implication is that Olbracht's readers must engage in a constant exercise of ideological decoding, cutting through rhetoric and self-deception to understand where power really lies. When the narrator says: "The gendarmes were helpless. They were frantic. They thrashed Eržika, they thrashed old Petr Šuhaj, they thrashed Ivan Dráč, they thrashed Nikola's brothers and sisters," the matter-of-fact delivery reinforces the cold-heartedness of the Czech police, even as the paradox of "helpless" yet violent gendarmes reflects their own self-pity and unselfconscious brutality. Marie K. Holeček's translation beautifully captures these subtle shifts in register and tone.

Nikola the Outlaw has never received the attention it deserves among English-speaking readers, even though the historian Eric Hobsbawm (who returned to this "remarkable" novel throughout his career) called it "the most moving and historically sound picture of social banditry I have come across."[1] Hobsbawm appreciated the enduring appeal of the bandit myth: Olbracht was dramatizing our desire for a just avenger to right all wrongs. At heart, however, Olbracht was too skeptical to be a mere mythmaker. (The one ideology he didn't see through was communism; he rejoined the party during World War II and lived out his life as a party functionary.) Instead, the fascination of reading the novel comes from seeing how skillfully Olbracht weaves back and forth *between* the romanticism of bandit tales and the skepticism of a disillusioned observer, someone who understands how politics can abuse language, legend, and desire.

Nikola the Outlaw refuses to dramatize an eternal battle of oppressor and oppressed or between the individual and the collective. Instead, it brilliantly depicts messy conflicts with many sharp edges, and characters who are confused, riven by conflicting emotions even as they are raked across the grain of state power. Nikola is a mountain spirit, a timeless symbol of rebellion. But he is also tangled up in the desperate fears and greed of his fellow townspeople and in the ambitions of a young state. There *are* no green boughs, just the magical tales we tell about them. What keeps *Nikola the Outlaw* compelling even today is this double vision, at once clear- and starry-eyed, reminding us that politics is powered by our fantasies, and rarely treats them well.

NOTE

1. E. J. Hobsbawm, *Primitive Rebels: Studies in Archaic Forms of Social Movement in the 19th and 20th Centuries* (Manchester: Manchester University Press, 1959), 14.

Chapter Twenty-Two

THE HOUSE OF HUNGER

DAMBUDZO MARECHERA

ISABEL HOFMEYR

CONTEMPORARY SOUTHERN Africa is littered with the detritus of grand schemes—imperialism, apartheid, development, independence, socialism. Wrought first by colonial violence and then by anticolonial movements gone bad, the wreckages of utopia heap up in Zimbabwe, Mozambique, Angola, and South Africa. The fallout of these schemes accumulates and compacts. Citizens find themselves making their lives on ideological as well as actual rubbish dumps.

The most acute diagnosis of this wreckage comes from the Zimbabwean Dambudzo Marechera, the writer of the garbage dump. Marechera grew up in colonial Rhodesia scavenging discarded books; in later years, he examined how certain lives get designated as disposable. His 1978 novella *House of Hunger*, published two years before Zimbabwean independence, is a kind of enteric nervous system, registering the processes of political waste making and the decomposition of the poor.

Fans of Marechera may be surprised to see *House of Hunger*, Zimbabwe's most famous work of fiction, in a B-Sides column. Given that his novella anticipates key moments of postcolonial theory—Achille Mbembe on the vulgarity of power in the postcolony, David Scott on the tragic time of postindependence sovereignty—Marechera's international reputation is surprisingly dim. Yet his view from the dump unmistakably pertains to our own time, when environmental catastrophe and waste making—first "pioneered" in the colony—are generalized across the world. A thinker who excoriated grand schemes, consistently identifying with the vagrant and the exile, Marechera would no doubt approve of being on the B-side.

As both a member and documenter of the precariat, Marechera was well acquainted with the bare-life logic of the camp and the dumping ground. Home was initially Vengere, the Black "location" (i.e., racially segregated residential area) of a tiny town, Rusape, in eastern Zimbabwe. After his father was killed in 1966, the family was evicted, and the fourteen-year old Marechera moved with his mother and eight siblings to a shanty town nearby, constructing a house out of mud and refuse.

His brilliance earned him entrance to the University of Rhodesia; student activism there made him a marked man. In 1974, Marechera fled the colony to take up a scholarship to New College, Oxford, but after spending eighteen months generally drunk, high, paranoid, absent from tutorials, and occasionally abusive and pyromaniacal, he was expelled. Once again, he entered bare life. He lived in tents, squats, doorways, even spent a few months in a Welsh prison.

In these depleted and often abject circumstances, his writing career began to take shape. His output was small—a short story collection, two novels, poetry, and a play—much of it published posthumously. With a powerful anarchist and experimental orientation, his corpus immediately caused ripples in orthodox African literary circles, then dominated by sober realism. Marechera's 1986 self-appraisal, much quoted, still rings true: "I am the doppelganger whom, until I appeared, African literature had not yet met."

House of Hunger was, by some accounts, written in exile in Oxford in a small tent alongside the River Isis. Yet its opening sentences forge a powerful connection between all dumping grounds, be they Third World locations and shantytowns or First World waste spaces: "I got my things and left. The sun was coming up. I couldn't think where to go. I wandered towards the beer hall but stopped at the bottle-store where I bought a beer . . . I couldn't have stayed on in that House of Hunger."

While ostensibly set in late colonial Rhodesia, the novella, or sections of it, could be about independent Zimbabwe. Black policemen prey on township residents; school children make their way to their indifferent schools. Bare life endures, under colonial rule and, as the novella anticipates, under the postindependence regime. Marechera elaborates the key challenge of postcolonial aesthetics, namely, what can be made from wreckage and ruin, a question that reverberates ever more loudly in our calamitous present.

Even as it opens, the narrative stalls. The unnamed narrator becomes mired at the bottle store, pursuing erratic conversations first with Harry, a school acquaintance and police informer, and then with Julia, possibly his girlfriend. Memories of childhood traumas, school cruelties, colonial brutalities, university persecutions, and failed romances crowd out the narrative present. Time appears to stutter and seize up. The messianic promise of liberation is overpowered by the reek and ruin of the township.

Freedom becomes another form of addiction: "The freedom we craved for—as one craves for dagga or beer or cigarettes or the after-life—this was so alive in our breath and in our fingers that one became intoxicated by it even before one had actually found it . . . the emptiness was deep-seated in the gut. We knew that before us lay another vast emptiness whose appetite for things living was at best wolfish. Life stretched out like a series of hunger-scoured hovels stretching endlessly towards the horizon . . . Gut-rot, that was what one steadily became."

Gut-rot refers both to cheap alcohol and to its corrosive effects on drinkers. Marechera is relating the historicity of the gut under colonial rule. This cheap alcohol was widely used in southern Africa to hook migrant laborers into addiction and endless contracts. To *become gut-rot* is to corrode the self as one corrodes others. There is no outside in this airless system, certainly no room for "disinterested intervention," something the narrator foolishly imagines he can manage in the triangular affair between him, his brother, and their object of desire, Immaculate.

House of Hunger—both the novella and the loosely linked stories that accompanied it when it came out in book form—is a prescient critique of militarized and masculinist authoritarianism. As Marechera saw back in the 1970s, the way in which one resists will be the way in which one is governed. The "black fist of power" will reproduce the violence that it claims to end; it "would fill up more lunatic asylums than it would swell the numbers of our political martyrs." The school bully Stephen is the intellectual representative of this militarized authoritarianism, evident in his admiration for a gallery of dictators: Nkrumah, Castro, Stalin, Mao.

The narrative ends with an old vagrant wandering in to tell aleatory stories of chameleons, dwarves, and fantastic happenings. He presents the narrator with a package that the informer Harry has dropped. It contains photographs of the protagonist and his friends with notes intended for the police. The novella comprises annotated portraits of the protagonist and his friends and so becomes yet another form of surveillance. There is no outside space of "disinterested intervention," only degrees of complicity in the system.

When Marechera returned to newly independent Zimbabwe in 1982, he was appalled by the prospect of life under a regime that quickly tried to ban one of his books as "offensive." This was an early sign of the political autoimmunity that the Zimbabwean regime would develop as it turned to attack its own citizens through ethnic cleansing and forced removals. Marechera had long foreseen this outcome and from the very beginning had cast scorn on Zimbabwean independence. Not content with heckling Robert Mugabe on his first postindependence visit to England, he doubled down on his defiance by arriving at a celebratory party dressed in aristocratic foxhunting gear.

Marechera steadfastly refused to align himself with the grand designs of the new nation, proclaiming that "my reading of intellectual anarchism reinforced my total hatred for a job which includes organizing human beings." Another, less celebrated line from that 1986 self-appraisal rings true: "I am aware of my vulnerability—that I am only me—and of my mortality; and that's why it seems to me always a waste of time to waste anybody's life in regulations, in ordering them." He dramatized his abjection by returning to a vagrant life, cadging off friends, living in temporary accommodation and on park benches.

Dambudzo Marechera died of AIDS in 1987, aged thirty-five. His lasting legacy is this somatically saturated work, one in which readers cannot escape the mind and body of the narrator. Bodies are broken, beaten, spat on, penetrated; they bleed, leak, and vomit over and over again, condemned to the wasting-time of the post/colony.

Chapter Twenty-Three

THE SHORT-TIMERS

GUSTAV HASFORD

STEVEN BIEL

THE MOST persistent source of anguish in war stories may be the inability to tell them: the sense of a vast experiential and moral distance between the battlefield and the home front. The gap between what we did over there and what they know about us back at home continues to stun returning soldiers. Today's anodyne phrase, "Thank you for your service," conveys the same sense of incommunicability and incomprehension—the impression of "a distance, a veil"—that the narrator, Paul Bäumer, recounted almost ninety years ago in *All Quiet on the Western Front.*

The recent wave of Iraq War fiction is as fixated on that gap as the novels of World War I. In *Billy Lynn's Long Halftime Walk*, Ben Fountain's protagonist is besieged by a "fervor" of self-congratulatory gratitude, by a relentless attack of thank-yous that bring tears to the eyes of the people uttering them, so full are they of "love for themselves and this tangible proof of their goodness." But that doesn't make his stateside reception any less "weird and frightening." In Phil Klay's story "Bodies," a marine who served in Mortuary Affairs reports the same experience: "I got home and everybody thanked me for my service. Nobody seemed to know exactly what they were thanking me for."

Joker, the narrator of Gustav Hasford's 1979 Vietnam War novel *The Short-Timers*, is perfectly aware of that veil between "in country" and "the World." What makes his story so startling, even all these years (and wars) later, is that he couldn't care less what we make of it. Joker addresses the World from in country, but he never agonizes over his or our understanding of what he has become. "In this world of shit you won't have time to understand," he counsels Rafter Man, a "New Guy" in the correspondents' corps at Da Nang. Joker's present-tense narration describes his hardening without sentiment, self-justification, or apology—with consciousness but without introspection. His detachment tells us all we need to know about how he "feels."

If you, like me, come to *The Short-Timers* after seeing Stanley Kubrick's 1987 adaptation, *Full Metal Jacket*, Hasford's Joker will look and sometimes sound like Matthew Modine. But there are crucial differences: the blandness of Modine's voiceover and his character's general befuddlement contrast with Joker's relentless and unsettling irony in the novel. When the deranged Leonard kills the drill sergeant who has tormented him in boot camp, the Joker of *The Short-Timers* doesn't shrink back in fear that he might be next. Instead, he calmly reflects on what has gone wrong in the process of turning this particular marine recruit into a killer: "Leonard is not hard enough to harness the power of an interior explosion to propel the cold black bullet of his will."

Hasford jumps from the boot camp scene ("The Spirit of the Bayonet") to Joker waiting for his next assignment, writing "upbeat news features" to pass along to civilian correspondents. He is bemused that Rafter Man "can still be touched" by the letters the USO delivers from "children back in the World"; to Joker, "the letters are like shoes for the dead, who do not walk." We learn that Joker has "been in the shit," but we don't get an account of what he has seen and done and how it has changed him, and he doesn't provide one to Rafter Man either.

"There it is," Joker and the other grunts often say. In *The Things They Carried* (1990), Tim O'Brien feels the need to furnish a translation of that enigmatic phrase: "Oh yeah, man, you can't change what can't be changed, there it is, there it absolutely and positively and fucking well *is*." Behind all his tough talk and cynical quips, that novel's narrator constantly struggles with his responsibility for participating in and adequately telling the "true war stories" that this talk and these jokes try to gloss over. Hasford's Joker, though, never bothers—or maybe it would be more accurate to say never condescends—to translate or explain. When he greets brutality with mordant humor, there is nothing behind it—no sensitive soul wanting sympathy, solace, or redemption.

Kubrick's film files off many of *The Short-Timer*'s rough edges. *Full Metal Jacket*'s Joker follows a trajectory from innocence to experience, or at least from softness to toughness; the battle of Hue serves as his rite of passage. In the film's climactic scene, the pursuit of a sniper in a decimated building, his rifle jams and he cowers behind a column while Rafter Man shoots the young woman. Mortally wounded, she pleads with the grunts to finish her off, and Joker reluctantly kills her. *The Short-Timers'* Joker doesn't betray fear when the sniper is poised to kill him, and he is matter-of-fact about killing her. "She recognizes me," he says, "I am the one who will end her life. We share a bloody intimacy." His friend Cowboy confirms what we already know: "Joker, that's a well done. You're hard." No rite of passage here. Joker is provocatively static in the novel, moving chronologically but not progressively through its incidents, counting down his days in country like the other soldiers who give *The Short-Timers* its title.

Kubrick's films are notoriously cold. *The Short-Timers* is colder. Its third section, "Grunts," vanishes from *Full Metal Jacket*, and it is not hard to see why. "Grunts" takes Joker to the siege of Khe Sanh, where another sniper picks off members of the squad. Cowboy is shot, and Joker must fulfill his obligation as a marine never to leave wounded comrades behind: "*Bang.* I sight down the short metal tube and I watch my bullet enter Cowboy's left eye. My bullet passes through his eye socket, punches through fluid-filled sinus cavities, through membranes, nerves, arteries, muscle tissue, through tiny blood vessels that feed three pounds of gray butter-soft high protein meat where brain cells arranged like jewels in a clock hold every thought and memory and dream of one adult male *Homo sapiens.*"

Then Joker tells a joke: a final verdict on his distance from the World, where "nobody asks us why we're smiling because nobody wants to know." He looks into the faces of the squad and says, "Man-oh-man, Cowboy looks like a bag of leftovers from a V.F.W. barbecue. Of course, I've got nothing against dead people. Why, some of my best friends are dead!" There it is.

Hasford took a line from Michael Herr's chilling *Dispatches* (1977) as the epigraph for "The Spirit of the Bayonet"—"I think that Vietnam was what we had instead of happy childhoods"— and Herr in turn collaborated with Kubrick on the screenplay for *Full Metal Jacket*. But Hasford's overlooked novel achieves something that sets him apart from both his Vietnam peers and recent chroniclers of Iraq: a verdict on war literature that goes beyond despair over the inadequacies of language, beyond even Hemingway's famous disavowal of "abstract words such as glory, honor, courage, or hallow" and embrace of the "dignity" of "the concrete names of villages, the numbers of roads, the names of rivers, the numbers of regiments and the dates."

Joker's narration recalls the voice of the anonymous grunt in *Dispatches* who not only dismisses the "overripe bullshit" of official euphemisms but also cuts through Herr's own literary self-consciousness—and any hope of salvaging dignity—with a vicious statement of the war's true purpose: "We're here to kill gooks. Period." When nobody really bothers to try to distinguish between enemy fighters and civilians, when "progress" can only be measured by body counts and "kill ratios," the evasions offered up by bureaucrats or politicians are obscenities, and writers' hand-wringing over how to bridge the gap between the war front and the home front is pointless. "Don't kid yourself, Rafter Man," Joker advises the New Guy. "This is a slaughter." Joker jokes, but he doesn't kid.

Chapter Twenty-Four

A FLAG FOR SUNRISE

ROBERT STONE

BEN FOUNTAIN

"**OH MY** fucking word," says elderly, rum-addled Father Egan. This is the first line of dialogue in Robert Stone's *A Flag for Sunrise* and a fair introduction to what follows: a violent, God-haunted intrigue set in the fictional Central American country of Tecan, circa 1977.

I sought out Stone's novel in desperation, you might say. By the time I first read it in the mid-1990s, I'd been hanging around Haiti for several years and started searching for writers who'd trod similarly fraught territory to help me make sense of what I was seeing. Haiti often resisted description, much less understanding; the disaster was too complete, too vast. The triumphant narrative of democracy, progress, and Christian values fell to pieces in the face of Haitian reality. One would have to go deeper, think better, and see sharper to get near the truth of the ravaged places of the world.

Stone and his brilliant novel showed how this might be done. Much like Nicaragua in the final years of the Somoza regime, the fictional Tecan—an obscenely impoverished and oppressed "disaster of history"—is about to blow. In the words of Sister Justin Feeney, née May Feeney of rural Idaho, who is fair, slender, and all of twenty-eight years old, the country will soon be "overrun by its inhabitants." A nursing nun in the midst of a full-blown crisis of faith, Sister Justin is, if not totally up to her ears in the revolutionary movement, sufficiently involved to attract the attention of the malevolent Guardia to herself and Father Egan. That's a dangerous development for the small medical mission they run in French Harbor, a tropical backwater on Tecan's Caribbean coast.

Trouble upon trouble: it's not only Lieutenant Campos of the Guardia who's drawn a bead on Sister Justin but the thugs of the local civilian power elite, too. Not to mention—God help her—the busy folks at CIA headquarters in Langley, Virginia. Over lunch in faraway New York, Frank Holliwell, a married, middle-aged professor of anthropology, is asked by his old CIA chum Marty Nolan to drop in on the mission in French Harbor. Nolan wants "insight" into the priest and nun. Since Holliwell's going to be in the neighborhood, giving a lecture at "the House of the Study of Mankind" in nearby Compostela, why not check them out? Nolan asks this as a favor between old friends, assuring Holliwell that this bit of casual spying will be for the missionaries' own good: they're surrounded by goons "who'd love nothing more than to mess with their private parts." "You might be in a position to help everybody out," Nolan says.

Holliwell's reply—"The last time I thought I was in that position things didn't work out very well"—makes explicit the connection between Tecan and a place across the world where Americans once made it their business to sway native hearts and minds. It was in Vietnam that Holliwell, then a young anthropologist working for USAID, did occasional favors for the CIA. That previous disaster hangs over the novel like a carcinogenic pall. As Holliwell reflects: "A great deal of profoundly fractured cerebration had gone down in Vietnam. People had been by turns Fascist mystics, Communist revolutionaries and junkies; at certain times, certain people had managed to be all three at once. It was the nature of the time—the most specious lunacy had been conceived, written, and enacted on both sides of the Pacific."

Readers—like a good many of Stone's own characters—suspect this special American lunacy is about to be repeated in Tecan. Such lunacy would in fact be reenacted over the course of the 1980s with American sponsorship of "dirty wars" in Nicaragua, Guatemala, Honduras, and El Salvador, as well as an outright invasion of Panama. And as for those goons who like to mess with people's private parts? Marty Nolan admits that "they're murderous troglodytes and we put them in," which raises the question of just what the American government thinks it's doing in Tecan, that we ally ourselves with thugs and torturers. Norman Mailer plumbed these same depths in books like *Why Are We in Vietnam?*, as did Joan Didion in her *Salvador* and *The Last Thing He Wanted*. They, like Stone, were onto something fundamental in the American character, a pathology that seems to have as much to do with profit taking as with paranoia.

"That is my subject," Stone said once, "America and Americans." Fighting commies, saving the world, serving the poor, making money, searching for God or love or meaning—whatever their motives, more than a few of the Americans in Tecan will be dead by the end. Stone serves up all the action and intrigue of a first-rate thriller (one of the plot lines involves a gun-running operation), but above all he's interested in the dark night of the soul, the existential crises that befall these Americans when they realize they're in over their heads. At that first lunch, Holliwell flatly refuses Nolan's CIA request, then, against his better judgment, goes to French Harbor anyway. This is his business, "his secret business, the business of his dry spirit," and once he meets Sister Justin he can't stay away. "He would find out what it was she believed herself to be about over there under the wooden cross."

Stone's other great subject, the religious impulse, cooks in these pages like water simmering a couple degrees shy of boiling. On one level—the geopolitical level—religion is the irksome wild card, the ghost in the machine. Close adherence to the Christian gospel is a poor match with paranoia and heedless profit taking, which is how an unarmed, relatively guileless American nun comes to be viewed by her own government as an enemy of the state. But Stone drills down into individual spiritual experience as well the workings of religion at ground level. Each in their own way, Stone's characters ache for a God who refuses to manifest. That yearning is active even in Pablo Tabor, a feral "Coast Guard deserter and speed freak" who perpetrates no fewer than four murders. Father Egan yearns for it; so do the dying Naftali and the hippies and burnouts who comprise Egan's vagabond flock. At evening they gather among Mayan ruins to hear him preach: "On the field of folk He is never at home, never available. Reach out a hand and there's only the terrifying touch of flesh, nothing firmer or finer. Ask questions and the answers are veiled in illusion, words from a fever dream."

The material world is too much with us, too much in us. "This is a dead place," Father Egan says. "It's a boneyard . . . It's history . . . It's the world." For Stone, this was most evident in the hot, green places of the world: Vietnam, Nicaragua, El Salvador, the Caribbean. At any rate, these were the places that drew him in, where the material world was most present, the things of the world too much with us.

Faith and salvation seem impossible amid the heat and fecundity of Tecan, yet at times the numinous lurks at the edges of sight, just out of focus. Sister Justin can no longer pray, but imagines she might see God in the faces of starving Tecanecans or in the eyes of the radical Father Godoy. For all her confusion of faith, Sister Justin remains so pure, so tragically frustrated, so uncompromising in her vocation, that Holliwell is drawn to the possibility of transcendence he senses in her: "She was different; she was heart, she was there, in there every minute feeling it. This kind of thing was not for him but he knew it when he saw it . . . It'll kill her, he thought, drive her crazy. Her eyes were already clouding with sorrow and loss. It was herself she was grieving and hoping for; for that reason she was the real thing. So he began to fall in love with her."

But she eludes him. Even after they've slept together, she eludes him. She sits up in bed with a bloodstained sheet wrapped around her and with a "cool despairing smile," recites these lines from Emily Dickinson:

A Wife—at Daybreak I shall be—
Sunrise—Hast thou a flag for me?

Whose wife? To whom or what does she belong? In the end, the country erupts and the goons bring Sister Justin to Lieutenant Campos, who destroys her with his fists and cattle prods. It's one of the grimmest scenes you'll ever encounter in American fiction, yet something seems to descend on Sister Justin in her grotesque suffering—an immanence, a glimmering, something "strong." "You after all? . . . You old destiny. You of Jacob, you of Isaac, of Esau. Let it be you after all. Whose after all I am." If this scene slants too much toward lurid melodrama—the vulnerable, saintly female at the mercy of male lust—Stone goes some way toward saving it by using the close third person point of view. As rendered from Sister Justin's perspective, the action is necessarily fractured and confused; the cheap satisfactions of a coherent, step-by-step account are denied the reader.

Stone's narrative acuity is such that he achieves a tragic prophecy in depicting Sister Justin's fate. Even as *A Flag for Sunrise* was being readied for publication, three American nuns and an American lay missionary were beaten, raped, and murdered in El Salvador by soldiers of the Salvadoran military: a military, it must be noted, that was trained, supplied, and enthusiastically supported by the U.S. government. Episodes of this kind became obscenely common throughout Central and Latin America in ensuing years.

No matter how common, these kinds of evil can never be allowed to seem "normal." We need writers like Stone to keep shocking us into consciousness, and that's the achievement of his merciless novel. Break your heart, this book. Leave you wrung out and gutted, as dazed as an earthbound angel dragging your mangled wings in the dirt, wind-sheared and shredded by American contrarieties. "I require rescue here," the nearly destroyed Frank Holliwell calls out at the end. Don't we all.

Chapter Twenty-Five

THE VEHEMENT PASSIONS

PHILIP FISHER

LORRAINE DASTON

ALL HISTORIANS develop a period ear. The faintest trace can anchor a text in its context: a whiff of anachronism, reversals in chronology, physiognomies of style and sentence length, wit tarnished by time, causes drained of urgency, allusions pointing nowhere. Works of scholarship and science age even more quickly than works of literature. A glance at the references usually suffices to date a book or article in both senses of the word: by year and by virtue of its musty obsolescence.

Rereading *The Vehement Passions* almost twenty years after I first encountered it, my period ear is confounded. Aside from obvious period markers—game theory and John Rawls, for instance—the book floats above time. In an era of humanistic scholarship made giddy by so many turns (the linguistic, the cultural, the material) taken at the speed of pirouettes, *The Vehement Passions* stands out as a steady alternative model of how to think with and about the humanities.

The passions singled out by the title—fear, anger, shame, grief, and wonder—are *vehement* in the sense of being sudden, strong, and episodic; *thorough* in the sense of saturating the self for as long as they last; and *time-defining* in the sense of carving out an extended now that includes the proximate past and the imminent future. When we are ambushed by fear, anger, or grief, the self fuses solid and all forms of split-consciousness—irony, ambivalence, doubt—evaporate. Such sieges of the soul know no nuance. Unlike the more pastel moods, the palette of the vehement passions is like that of medieval stained-glass windows: sky-blue, grass-green, and blood-red.

In Fisher's telling, the literary and philosophical heritage of these vehement passions is ancient and enduring; it stretches back to Homeric epic and persists through the evolutionary and physiological theories of Charles Darwin, William James, and beyond. He takes this sturdy tradition to be prima facie evidence of "a sustained core account of human nature in spite of the constructions of culture, power, and historical moment, and for the deep structural grasp on certain themes within the changing episodes and local design or redesign that can be traced in our three-thousand-year record."

It is tempting to herald Fisher's riveting exploration of the vehement passions as a forerunner of the current trend of affect theory, as a history of certain emotions. But neither "history" nor "emotions" quite fits Fisher's magisterial essay on how a handful of gripping states have provided the template (his word) for thinking about all affective experience and even what it means to have an experience.

"Emotions" first: one of the many intellectual delights of this book is the surgical delicacy with which Fisher probes our slapdash vocabulary for affect. After reading Fisher's analysis of why past attempts to classify the emotions neatly into groups and pairs were an exercise in futility, one regards the current taxonomies of affect theory with a healthy skepticism. The stun-gun passions (which has the same root as "patient," or, one who suffers rather than possesses a state of body and mind) have little in common with the perturbations of the Stoics or the commotions of the Enlightenment and much less to do with the wan moods (boredom) and sentiments (nostalgia) of the nineteenth century. Feelings we may own, like the contents of our cupboards. Passions, on the contrary, own us.

As these sharp distinctions among the terms we habitually conflate indicate, Fisher's analysis is by no means ahistorical despite the universalist overtones of that promise of "a sustained core account of human nature." But it is history in a different vein from that practiced by most historians of the emotions—or historians, tout court—writing today. For one thing, Fisher doesn't bind himself to the chunks of time and space that circumscribe context for most historians: "Victorian Britain," "republican China," "medieval Sicily," for example. His sources are selective—mostly philosophical and literary and exclusively Western—but wide-ranging, from Aristotle to Baudelaire, Sophocles to Proust. If his erudition was not so unobtrusive, it would be staggering by current specialist standards. For another, his emphasis is on continuity. Fisher certainly notes key inflection points: Stoic (and later Christian) attempts to cure the passions as if they were diseases, the "spiritualization" of fear and wonder into the complacent frisson of the sublime by Kant and the Romantics. Yet at a time when most humanists make "complicate" their motto and take it as their mission to reveal the teeming diversity of human experience in order to stave off the universalism of the biologists and economists, Fisher excavates regularities and aims to simplify.

Beneath the surface variability of three millennia, beneath diverse vocabularies and traditions, Fisher discovers deeper, consequential patterns. The "paths" he maps among the vehement passions draw attention to persistent trajectories among them that are of potential interest to the physiologist and the lawyer alike, as well as the philosopher and the literary scholar. Fear passes into shame, jealousy into rage—but rarely in the other direction. As Fisher remarks, it is unsurprising that a high-intensity passion ends in exhaustion, but "why within the long episode of exertion should some but not other combinations be possible, and possible in one direction only?" This is an observation fertile in hypotheses that beg to be tested. Fisher's brilliant analysis of how and why the vehement passions distort the smooth flow of time by staking out a privileged zone of the near past and the near future is a trenchant critique of accounts of rationality within philosophy, game theory, and neoclassical economics. More than just critique, this careful account of how time dilates and contracts under the influence of the vehement passions clears the way for a more contextual and empirically accurate explanation of decision making and risk taking in moments of extremity.

Fisher's inquiry into the vehement passions is mostly phenomenological—although open to explanations from the sciences, he prudently refrains from neuroscientific or evolutionary speculation. Yet there is nothing "mere" about his descriptions. Rich in suggestive and often striking observations, the implications of Fisher's inquiry cut straight across current divisions of knowledge. His brand of empiricism simultaneously supplements, complements, and sometimes corrects that of the laboratory and the field. At the present hand-wringing moment, this is a model for the humanities that leads rather than follows. Still illuminating and surprising after twenty years, it defies the period ear.

PART V

HOME FIRES

HOME: WHEN you go there, they have to let you in. Only, then what happens? To the beloved fantasy writer Ursula K. Le Guin, John Galt's two-century-old *Annals of the Parish* offers up "a good place to spend a few quiet hours, these days, and have an excellent dinner." Sharon Marcus proposes that Shirley Jackson's domestic sketches imagine home as the natural locus of farce, where "regress rules over progress [and] any attempt to solve the smallest problem only makes it worse." In *The Dry Heart*, Merve Emere hears Natalia Ginzburg asking a simple question over and over: *"When should a woman kill her husband?"*

Pardis Dibashi's appreciation of *My Uncle Napoleon* brings out the pathos of being consigned to merely domestic life: how terribly distant it can feel from the places that matter, where politicians and oil companies divvy up the spoils. Elizabeth Graver thinks it is the miniaturization of Edward Jones's short stories that makes them sublime. She praises the way he carves out space and time for even the minorest of minor characters to have "a story; in one sentence, we glimpse its comedy, its force, its cosmic arc." Kevin Brazil loves how A. J. Ackerley's *We Think the World of You* conveys at once the joy of belonging (by caring for the beloved's dog) and the inescapable bitterness of feeling that the very idea of belonging is not for the likes of you.

Chapter Twenty-Six

ANNALS OF THE PARISH

JOHN GALT

URSULA K. LE GUIN

FOR THIRTY or forty years a book has been lurking on my shelves, a beautiful little Everyman's Library edition published by Dent and Dutton, undated, with red fake leather binding and real gold leaf lettering and ornamentation on the spine and front cover: *Annals of the Parish*. Last spring, looking for a novel to read, any novel so long as it wasn't a dystopia, I saw it and remembered I'd bought it ages ago in England and never yet had read it. A truly, undeservedly forgotten book, if perhaps not exactly a great one.

The author, John Galt, born in Ayrshire in Scotland in 1779, was an ambitious entrepreneur who founded the city of Guelph in Canada; an honest, generous, partly successful businessman; and a prolific, uneven writer. A friend and biographer of Byron, he was a contemporary of both Walter Scott and Jane Austen. And I started *Annals of the Parish* expecting something like Scott, but very soon I was thinking, "This is like Jane Austen!"

Now that's very rare. Nobody, really, is like Jane Austen. Her style and sensibility were thoroughly of her time and age and class, but her voice and her art are singularly incomparable. And Galt certainly has none of Austen's brilliance, her reach of mind, her diamond flash of wit. But his humor, though softer, is like hers—dry, subtle, morally loaded, and really funny. It may be characteristically Scottish, but it reminds me of the western American humor that's so understated, so quiet and peaceful-seeming that you can go on for quite a ways before you realize that you just got shot dead.

And then Galt began to remind me of another writer, Elizabeth Gaskell, particularly her *Cranford*, which like *Annals* is the portrait of a town. From Hardy's Casterbridge to Thomson's Lark Rise, from Jewett's Dunnet Landing to Lewis's Gopher Prairie and Haruf's Holt, small-town novels are intensely grounded; rich in satire, humor, and character, human affectations and affections. Intimate knowledge of one small community may yield psychological and anthropological insights of universal value.

Many small-town novels began as short stories and remain loose in structure, episodic—*Cranford*, though a miraculous work of art, is only halfway to being a novel by the end. As for *Annals of the Parish*, it's exactly what it says it is: the annual records of Mr. Balwhidder, minister of the parish of Dalmailing in Ayrshire, kept and dated year by year for fifty years, from 1760 to 1810.

Mr. Balwhidder is a very old-fashioned narrator and therefore reliable. He will not, he cannot, mislead you. He is transparent. He is as honest as the day is long and as naive as a man can be. I can best describe him as an innocent heart.

Whatever his annals tell of greed, cruelty, or hate is perceived in a way now very rare in literature, if it exists at all. Violence is witnessed *without participation*. The first event in the first year of the *Annals* is a violent one—an attack on Mr. Balwhidder by parishioners opposed to his installation as their minister. As he goes to his first service in his church, an angry crowd closes round him yelling and throwing clods at him. He finds the door of the kirk nailed shut and has to clamber in at the window. The mob follows him in with "grievous yellyhooing." Riot continues inside the kirk. His induction as minister is an insulting travesty. All he says about it is, "I thought I would have a hard and sore time of it with such an outstrapolous people." And: "After the ceremony, we then got out at the window, and it was a heavy day to me; but we went to the manse, and there we had an excellent dinner."

Having read that sentence, I was in love with the book. In pure, ignorant defiance of the decree of the Iowa Writing School that controls almost all modern fiction, Galt *tells without showing*. No blow-by-blow, in-your-face, gut-wrenching description of the young minister forced to climb out the window of his new church amid the jeers and threats of a hateful crowd, the fear, the humiliation. We are not forced to participate in the violence. It's left up to us to hear what's being told, to imagine it, to feel it. And all the material we need in order to hear, imagine, feel the scene is in those few words, in their choice and in their cadence. Galt's prose works like poetry:

every word *tells*. "We then got out at the window, and it was a heavy day to me."

And immediately, without even a period, only a semicolon, "we went to the manse, and there we had an excellent dinner." This is a man to whom violence and hatred is so foreign it doesn't really touch him. He's had a fearful, shameful beginning to his ministry; it was a heavy day to him; but must a bad day ruin a good dinner? Mr. Balwhidder, for all his innocence, is a strong man, whose soul is in good balance. We can laugh at him without the least disrespect.

Slow-paced, very quiet in tone, and hardly more than a novella in length, this little novel recounts a man's long lifetime, portrays a whole community, and lets us see the American Revolution, the French Revolution, and the Napoleonic Wars through the eyes of ordinary people—from the mothers of boys who enlist as soldiers, to Mr. Cayenne, a rich American plantation owner whose fierce allegiance to his king, George III, has driven him into self-exile in Scotland.

None of the characters, indeed, can be dismissed as ordinary. Most of them (including Mr. Balwhidder, and the two Mrs. Balwhidders) are occasionally admirable, occasionally ridiculous. Some of them do a good deal of harm, yet not one is merely evil—nor, however benevolent, purely good. This world is a complicated place, nothing is simple, nothing can be taken for granted.

Yet for all that, the air is very clear in this corner of Scotland, just rounding the corner of the century toward the stormy extremes of Romanticism. A good place to spend a few quiet hours, these days, and have an excellent dinner.

Chapter Twenty-Seven

THE DRY HEART

NATALIA GINZBURG

MERVE EMRE

WHEN SHOULD a woman kill her husband?

I have turned this question over and over in my mind since reading Natalia Ginzburg's *The Dry Heart*, a grim, anti-Romantic novella about marriage and betrayal. It opens with a bang.

> "Tell me the truth," I said.
>
> "What truth?" he echoed. He was making a rapid sketch in his notebook and now he showed me what it was: a long, long train with a big cloud of black smoke swirling over it and himself leaning out of a window to wave a handkerchief.
>
> I shot him between the eyes.

Ginzburg's narrator will return to the scene of her crime several times to fill in the details. She is the wife, unnamed.

He is her husband, Alberto. Their marriage has been pocked by his infidelity and her unhappiness, by the death of their child and their inability to conceive another. Her suffering is laid out on the first page of the novella in a tone that is controlled, unsentimental, precise, and committed to the inevitability— the necessity—of shooting her husband. "But for a long time already I had known that sooner or later I should do something of the sort." The only problem left to resolve is the time of death. Why kill him now? Why not sooner or later?

I have a theory that the sudden onset of unusual events— affairs, murders, suicides, deliverances—receives its most intense treatment in the novella. It is a genre that compresses, with terrible and dazzling force, the violent human entanglements that the novel unravels over a longer span of time. In the German Romantic *Novellen* of Kleist and Novalis, which Ginzburg nods to throughout, the machinery for producing all manner of high-octane emotions is focused repetition. By narrating a single event over and over, each time disclosing a little more detail or dialogue, the author expands plot and characterization around a frozen center. That moment, stopped in time, begins to quiver with anticipation, with narrative possibility.

Reading *The Dry Heart* is like listening to a person confess in half-truths. The second time the narrator revisits killing Alberto, she describes how she prepared him a thermos of tea with milk and sugar before pulling his revolver out of his desk. The third time, she reveals that he was packing his bags for a trip; that she suspected he was not traveling alone; and that when she told him she would "rather know the truth, whatever it may be," he replied by misquoting Dante's *Purgatorio*: "She seeketh Truth, which is so dear / As knoweth he who life for her refuses."[1] The final time, he laughs at her before she pulls the trigger.

We learn that husband and wife have played out their goodbye many times before, never getting any closer to the truth, suspended in a purgatory of weakness, indecision, loneliness, and self-deception. Alberto often leaves on holidays with his lover, Giovanna, but always returns. Insisting that he respects his wife too much to lie to her, he complains about Giovanna's deception and inconstancy, holding up his torment for the narrator's inspection as if offering her some rare, precious stone. "We've said all sorts of cruel things to each other and given up the affair completely," he confesses. "Then we've come together again, and every time, even after so many years, it's like something brand new." But what is "brand new" for Alberto cannot be made new for his wife. His repetition converts her agony into tedium, a diminishment that the novella, with its commitment to intense feelings, cannot sustain. The only way to honor the genre's conventions is to stop Alberto from doing what he cannot stop himself from doing—boring us.

When should a woman kill her husband? One answer: when there's nothing left to do with him, narratively speaking.

There's nothing much to do with Alberto, who is not an unusual or especially interesting man. "He said that he was like a cork bobbing on the surface of the sea, pleasantly cradled by the waves but unable to know what there was at the bottom," the narrator recalls of the only conversation during their courtship in which Alberto talks about himself. Though she feels unsatisfied—his words "amounted to very little," she admits—his evocation of the waves and the sea, of the unknown and perhaps unknowable depths of being, spurs her lonely imagination to what she thinks is love. The sensitive quality of his speech animates her desire to know more about his inner life, to "get to the bottom of things and turn them over and over" in the belief that her excavation will be rewarded.

But rewarded with what? Not love and not desire—not exactly. Before they get married, the thought of sleeping with Alberto fills her with "terror and disgust." He is old, short, ratty, and, predictably, bad in bed. When they make love, she consoles herself with the "tender, feverish words" he whispers in the dark. But she soon discovers that Alberto's repertoire is limited. Repeating the same words too many times drains them of their meaning, their capacity to delight and intrigue. The cork resurfaces twice, first when Alberto tells the narrator that he still loves Giovanna: "He said she was often unkind to him and his life was entirely without joy. He felt stupid and useless, like a cork bobbing on the water." The second time, it is as a metaphor and accusation delivered by the narrator: "You're a cork bobbing on the surface, that's what you are." The original simile suddenly, startlingly, loses its depth. Alberto is exposed as a hollow, passive, discardable thing.

Alberto's hollowness and passivity emerge from his commitment to a specific form of unreality: literature. Few of the words he speaks belong to him. He echoes others, quotes books. His entire being is on loan from the Romantics: from the poems of Rilke, which he reads aloud to both his wife and Giovanna; from the writings of Goethe, which supply the emotional template for his tortured longing. When Alberto and his friend Augusto both fall in love with Giovanna, they buy matching revolvers and vow to commit suicide—a joint performance of the ending of *The Sorrows of Young Werther*. He spends evenings dictating to his wife the notes he has written in the margins of his books for a volume he calls, after a line in *Faust*, *Variations on a Minor Scale*. Lest we doubt Ginzburg's anti-Romantic bent, *The Dry Heart* even takes its title from an overwrought speech in Goethe's *Elective Affinities*. "Leave me alone—you who have a dry heart and dry eyes!" says a weeping man bewildered by his attraction to a young, beautiful woman who is not his wife. "I curse the happy for whom the unhappy is only a spectacle." Nearly two hundred years after Romanticism flared out, Alberto's performance of powerlessness is only that, a spectacle—anachronistic, self-aggrandizing, false.

When should a woman kill her husband? Another answer: when killing him is no more a violation than killing off a stock character, an assemblage of someone else's words.

The Dry Heart ends with the narrator composing her confession in the notebook where she keeps track of the household expenses. As she transforms the notebook from a ledger of domestic unhappiness into something more, perhaps the very novella we are reading, she pauses: "All of a sudden I asked myself for whose benefit I was writing." For most of her married life, the narrator has addressed only herself or Alberto with reproach and regret. Now she is free to address whomever she wants and however she wants—to shape a collective consciousness. Yet the precise figuration of her audience eludes her. Is it Giovanna? Is it her mother? "It was too difficult to decide," she concludes.

But the decision is so obvious it doesn't need to be stated. The narrator writes for the benefit of any woman trapped in someone else's story as an auxiliary character: the suffering wife or the strung-along lover. Turning the wife into both narrator and protagonist gives her control over the story's events, pacing, tone, point of view, and genre. It lets her call the shots.

The choice of the novella, then, offers a cool, impatient response to novel-length performances of male indecision, self-absorption, and sentimentality. (If Alberto were the narrator, the book would be called *Alberto's Way*, and you better believe there would be five more volumes to read.) Ginzburg, an antifascist, a feminist, and the first translator of *Swann's Way* into Italian, writes for any woman eager to fit her bourgeois unhappiness to a form that can accommodate a quick and definitive ending.

When should a woman kill her husband? Final answer: when it's the only way to free yourself.

NOTE

1. "He seeketh Liberty . . . " (Dante, *Purgatory*, 1.71).

Chapter Twenty-Eight

LIFE AMONG THE SAVAGES; RAISING DEMONS

SHIRLEY JACKSON

SHARON MARCUS

ANYONE WHO has spent at least three hours in sole charge of two or more children has stories to tell but few faculties left with which to tell them. Luckily, we have a genre—I'll call it "domestic farce"—that documents the trials and tribulations of family life. Major contributors to this minor mode include George Grossmith, Jean Kerr, Erma Bombeck, and Dave Barry. Towering above them is the genre's midcentury modern foremother: Shirley Jackson.

Today, most people know Jackson as the author of the much-anthologized tale "The Lottery," in which a mundane village gathering turns horrific in the story's final lines. That 1948 *New Yorker* publication won Jackson instant notoriety and set the tone for two critically acclaimed neo-Gothic novels, *The Haunting of Hill House* (1959) and *We Have Always Lived in the Castle* (1962).

During Jackson's lifetime, however, she was equally famous for vignettes of quirky family life, first published in women's magazines then anthologized as *Life Among the Savages* (1953) and *Raising Demons* (1957). They tell the story of a New York City wife and mother transplanted to rural Vermont, where she contends with rambunctious children, strong-willed pets, and uncooperative household objects.

Each story vanquishes chaos through style. Turning mundane drudgery into the stuff of comedy, Jackson makes much of life's smallest problems in order to make light of them. Farce has a reputation for crude exaggeration, but its choreographed mayhem requires careful planning and skill. The verbal misunderstandings, antic entrances and exits, pratfalls and pie throws on which this comic genre thrives depict loss of control with perfect control. In the hands of writers such as Oscar Wilde, Joe Orton, and Shirley Jackson, farce enacts the triumph of formally ordered art over anarchic life—not by containing the mess but by orchestrating it with wicked precision.

A typical farce usually features at least one scene that squeezes many disparate characters into small spaces. Jackson's tales often jam four very different children, eager to battle their parents and one another, into houses, cars, and trains. Here they are, about to embark on a family trip from Vermont to New York:

> It has long been my belief that in times of great stress, such as a four-day vacation, the thin veneer of family unity wears off almost at once, and we are revealed in our true personalities; Laurie, for instance, is a small-town mayor, Jannie a

Games mistress, Sally a vague stern old lady watching the rest of us with remote disapproval, and Barry a small intrepid foot soldier, following unquestioningly and doggedly. The two nervous creatures hovering in the background, making small futile gestures and tending to laugh weakly, are, of course, unmistakable. They are there to help with the luggage.

Jackson's light irony deftly equates "vacation" with a time of "great stress," but her confident marshaling of commas and semicolons belies the ineffectuality she attributes to her parental characters. Her clauses glide forward with all the smoothness missing from the contentious, lurching train ride that follows.

In serious literature, characters mature as they confront world-historical forces. In farce, regress rules over progress. Any attempt to solve the smallest problem only makes it worse, and we laugh at the human will's failure to overcome even the tiniest obstacles. One episode starts as a search for a lost sneaker ("day after day after day I went around my house picking things up") and ends almost exactly where it began: the first shoe found, but its companion misplaced.

Farce thrives on comic pileups, and Jackson excels at household inventories whose sheer length makes them list hilariously out of proportion. "I picked up books and shoes and toys and socks and shirts and gloves and boots and hats and handkerchiefs and puzzle pieces and pennies and pencils and stuffed rabbits and bones the dogs had left under the living room chairs." Just when you think the pileup has to end, it resumes:

"I also picked up tin soldiers and plastic cans and baseball gloves and sweaters and children's pocketbooks with nickels inside and little pieces of lint off the floor."

In a genre whose every rule inverts the principles governing tragedy and epic, lesser forces ruthlessly prevail over more august ones. The inorganic thwarts the organic, the childish circumvents the mature, small creatures run rampant while larger ones helplessly observe them. Jackson's adults are no match for the recalcitrant objects that surround them: refrigerator doors that won't open, cars and furnaces that won't start, children with minds of their own. Chapters often begin with the maternal narrator recounting the difficulty she has simply getting herself or her offspring into or out of bed, washed, dressed, seated at a table, settled on a car or train.

In one story, mice appear, popping out of kitchen drawers, eating salted almonds from a living room dish, running down the narrator's arm via a ceiling light cord. The family dog flees in terror; the cats leave the room, indignant at having their rest disturbed. The narrator's four children vote to adopt a third cat *and* a puppy in the hope that new pets will put up a better fight. The result: even more animals bursting through doors and eating food intended for others. As she often does, Jackson gives a child the punch line: "Why'd we *get* all these cats and dogs, anyway?" Sally asked. "Seems like it would be easier just having *mice* for pets."

Humor is often a weapon of the weak, and readers of *Life Among the Savages* and *Raising Demons* may wonder whether Jackson's comedy is meant to mask rage. Sometimes it does, particularly when directed at the narrator's husband, who can't feed himself a cracker, controls every penny his wife spends while indulging a passion for coin collecting, and assumes that his young daughter will sew his shirt buttons when his wife is out of town. Jackson's farce, though, is more than an outlet for muted resentment. As Ruth Franklin points out in her authoritative biography, these stories also communicate Jackson's genuine pleasure in her brood, whose inventive imaginations and linguistic wit mirror her own.

The mundane chaos Jackson portrays in *Life Among the Savages* and *Raising Demons* amuses and comforts us because the author bends time, space, and creaturely life to her writerly will with a mastery equal to the forces that defy her protagonist. The heroine of a domestic farce aims less at getting over her antagonists than at momentarily getting on top of them. Jackson's impeccable comic technique makes light of everyday difficulties as a wrestler makes light of an opponent. Characters may struggle, but the author stands above the fray. For the precious moments we spend reading these books, we stand above it with her.

Chapter Twenty-Nine

MY UNCLE NAPOLEON

IRAJ PEZESHKZAD

PARDIS DABASHI

IN THE central courtyard, in the middle of a family party, in midcentury Tehran, a fart rings out. Or *was* it a fart? A cat? A cat's fart? The sound of a chair being dragged across the stone ground? Solving this riddle means calling on Deputy Taymur Khan and drawing examining magistrate Shamsali Mirza out of retirement. The absurd lengths to which the family goes in pursuit of this "dubious sort of sound" epitomizes the naughty hilarity of Iraj Pezeshkzad's 1973 novel, *My Uncle Napoleon*.

Among other works, Pezeshkzad wrote *Mashalah Khan in the Court of Harun al-Rashid* (1971) and some bitingly satirical essays about the Islamic Republic of Iran. But *Napoleon*, adapted into a wildly popular television series in the late 1970s, is by far his most famous work. The story unfolds from the viewpoint of the novel's nameless narrator, a teenage boy who is in love with his cousin Layli—he is desperate to prevent her being married off to their other cousin, Shapur. The main problem is Layli's father, nicknamed "Dear Uncle Napoleon" for his obsession with the French emperor Bonaparte, with whom he feels a spiritual affinity. Dear Uncle (in Persian, *Da'i Jan*) has nothing but disdain for his sister's husband, "an ordinary person" from "the provinces." Alas, for our narrator, that mere provincial is his father.

This story of thwarted young love, though, only paves the way for the novel's real subject: Uncle Napoleon's political paranoia. The "dubious sort of sound" heard in the family courtyard in the novel's opening pages becomes an object of investigation because Dear Uncle thinks it may be a sign that the British are coming after him. Dear Uncle is convinced not only that the British are plotting against him personally (for having fought against them during World War I) but also that they are behind any and all calamitous events in Iran's modern history and political present.

Dear Uncle has a point. During most of the nineteenth century, Iran was a pawn in Russia's, Britain's, and France's competitive colonial projects, and by the fin de siècle, Britain had control of large portions of Iranian infrastructure. While Britain did not officially colonize Iran, it nevertheless exploited its resources (initially tobacco, subsequently oil) by manipulating the brutal and corrupt Qajar monarchy. Uncle Napoleon's conspiracy theories would certainly have resonated with the novel's first readers, in the 1970s, who would have recognized the continuation of British influence right up into the reign of the shah. Even paranoids, as they say, have enemies.

Pezeshkzad's novel is about what it means to be absolutely convinced that hidden machinations are taking place beyond

one's ken. Dear Uncle is both the protagonist of the novel and
a minor character; he is the center around which the novel's
cacophony of events takes place, though rarely their primary
actor. Dear Uncle's convoluted imagination is symptomatic of
a peripheral existence: knowing that political schemes are
being hatched but able to experience them only at a distance,
he turns to tall tales as a way of regaining control.

It makes perfect sense, then, that Uncle Napoleon and his
faithful servant, Mash Qasem—with whom he forms a Don
Quixote–and–Sancho Panza–esque duo—claim, falsely, to
have fought in the Constitutional Revolution of 1906–1911.
And that they tell everyone within earshot that, during World
War I, they fought valiantly against the British in the Battles
of Mamasani and Kazerun, changing the number of British
they killed with each telling.

Ultimately, Dear Uncle is not wrong that the British are
exercising control over Iranian politics—even if his stories
about how that control occurs are, in their specifics, sheer fic-
tions. But he is also not wrong in another, more immediate
sense. Plots *are* taking place around him, and they often *are*
happening at his expense, but simply in a different way than he
expects.

Upon learning, for instance, that Uncle Napoleon is planning to take his family away from Tehran to escape the
encroaching British, the narrator and his friend, foreign ministry official (and bawdy trickster) Asadollah Mirza, ask for the
help of their new neighbor, an Indian man they come to call
"Brigadier Maharat Khan." Uncle Napoleon is suspicious that
the Brigadier is a British agent sent to spy on him. Knowing

this, the narrator and Asadollah use the Brigadier as a pawn to sabotage Dear Uncle's intended departure, since the narrator can't imagine being separated from Layli.

Asadollah hatches a plan: he will disclose to the Brigadier that Uncle Napoleon is leaving for a trip to Nayshapur by way of Qom. The Brigadier is to bid Dear Uncle goodbye on the day he plans to leave and, "during the course of the conversation to mention, casually and naturally as it were, the name of the town Nayshapur." This way, Uncle Napoleon will be confirmed in his suspicions that the Brigadier is a spy and will stay put in Tehran. Asadollah's tactic works—the Brigadier slips the word "Nayshapur" casually into conversation with Dear Uncle. Dear Uncle is subsequently thrown into a panic and determines to secure help from the Germans to fend off what he now knows, without a shadow of a doubt, is the scheming of "these English wolves" to wage "a war of nerves against [him]." This he does by way of a secret code involving the phrase, "My late grandfather is eating *ab-gusht* [mutton stew] with Jeanette McDonald"—a sentence each of us should find reason to say at least once in our lifetime.

Pezeshkzad turns this penchant for ludic invention into something more than mere political allegory; it becomes a covert organizing principle for the novel as a whole. Qamar, the narrator's cousin, gets pregnant out of wedlock, so the family has to cover it up by marrying her to a bald man they force to wear a wig; the family has to fend off the local butcher, who's come to kill one of the cousins for having cuckolded him; the narrator kicks Shapur in the groin, rendering his genitals temporarily inoperative; and so on and so forth. Lacking any real dramatic ramifications, these boisterous vignettes simply proliferate, calling attention to their own fictionality.

The novel is not, however, altogether plotless. Dear Uncle dies of cardiac complications brought on by a nervous breakdown, but not before fulfilling his dying wish that Layli be married to Shapur. The narrator's heartache sends him first to the hospital, then to Beirut with Asadollah till after World War II, then to Paris, and finally back to Tehran. We learn in an epilogue that the narrator is writing the novel's last lines from Geneva. (Food for thought: Pezeshkzad's own first love was a young woman whose well-to-do father disapproved of him, and he himself currently lives and writes in Paris.)

I was awfully young when my father urged me to read *My Uncle Napoleon*. "It's one of the funniest things you'll ever read," he said. His recommendations had been right before (*The Adventures of Huckleberry Finn*, *Northanger Abbey*, *Great Expectations*), but at ten I was put off by *Napoleon*'s length and never even began. Arriving at it two decades later, I experienced a strange form of recognition, a moment of cognitive reorientation or contact. Unbeknownst to me, a whole fictional world had been sitting in my father's head. Now I too had arrived there. And though this world was full of invented stories, false in all their details, I nevertheless felt I had come to know something fantastically true.

Chapter Thirty

WE THINK THE WORLD OF YOU

J. R. ACKERLEY

KEVIN BRAZIL

J. R. ACKERLEY'S *We Think the World of You* (1960) isn't a novel I'd ever say I think the world of, maybe because it has taught me how little the world can amount to. The story opens with a bachelor civil servant called Frank visiting his friend Johnny in jail. "'I'm so sorry, Johnny,' I said. 'It couldn't be 'elped, Frank,' he replied." The class divide between them is as unspeakable as Johnny's dropped aitches make it unmistakable. Something else unspeakable hangs over this visit, as well. Frank is in a prison of his own with Johnny, "unwilling to assist him, unable to give him up."

And so while Johnny serves out his sentence, Frank pays for the upkeep of Johnny's wife, Megan, and their three children in order to remind Johnny that she isn't the only one who loves him. "Vile Megan" is Frank's nemesis in a war for Johnny's affection, a war intensified because, as his legal spouse, Megan is the only one who has an automatic right to visit Johnny in prison and the only who can decide to give up a precious visit to someone else. There is, though, one thing Frank can do to help Johnny in prison—take care of his dog, Evie. "I think the world of 'er," Johnny says, making who thinks what about Evie central to Frank's quest to gain one more visit.

As a respectable civil servant living in 1950s England, Frank can't tell anyone why he thinks the world of Johnny. Because he is the novel's only narrator, he can't tell us either. And so in bounds Evie, the most overdetermined dog in the history of canine symbolism. She doesn't bound very much at first because she is living with Johnny's mother, Millie, in her cramped terraced house. But taking Evie for walks soon becomes a way for Frank to maintain the imprisoned Johnny's affection. More than that, it becomes a way for Johnny's affection for Frank to be recognized, for Millie to be able to say: "Oh yes, he thinks the world of you, Frank."

Becoming Evie's sole walking companion also allows Frank to have what he really wants: something of Johnny's that Megan can't have—a visit of his own. Johnny, he laments, "ought to *take away* from her and *give* to me, *give* me something for myself"; the couple "ought to make a sacrifice." But while Frank takes Evie on walks through a bombed-out East End, something unexpected arises: he comes to identify with her. There she sits, trapped in Millie's house, beaten by Millie's husband, languishing "day after day, nothing, nothing; the giving and the never getting; the hoping and the waiting for something that never comes."

Frank also comes to enjoy Evie's affection, the kind given across the unequal divide between animal and human. Nothing in this novel, though, is uncomplicated: Evie reveals herself to be "a bully and a nag." She has one overriding desire, one that Frank ought to recognize: "to get me to herself"—all to herself. She demands to be taken to his office in Whitehall, she attacks any colleague who vies for his attention, she attacks him for avoiding her. A love so selfish is impossible to receive: Evie must be betrayed. Frank tries to dispatch her to a dog home in leafy Surrey. Alas, Millie finds out and temporarily severs all contact between Frank and Evie.

Frank recoils from Evie because he realizes her desires are all-demanding: "Her meat was finished and mine too, for I had given her my week's ration; how could I shop for more?" Yet he too has an all-demanding desire: to take Johnny from Megan and have him to himself. Frank is trapped in his own version of postwar Britain's strict regime of rationing. He is given tacit permission to pursue Johnny—a stingy off-cut—but only on the condition that he renounces his desire to have his relationship publicly acknowledged—the prime fillet steak, as it were. This sort of rationing (we also call it the closet) traps Frank inside a vault of his own selfishness. Because he is forced to sacrifice, he can only imagine that he is receiving love when someone is sacrificing something for him.

And so Evie reveals the cruel irony at the heart of the novel: Frank is as unwilling to sacrifice the little comforts of his world for Evie as Johnny is unwilling to sacrifice his world for Frank. Yet Frank cannot see himself as overly demanding like the unappeasable Evie; he can only see himself as the Evie who gives but never gets.

Readers, though, can see everything that Evie means. In a novel where what Frank is cannot be named, she is the only way the other characters can negotiate what he wants. She is the suffering dog Frank identifies with, the selfish animal he recoils from, a part of Johnny he wants taken from Megan, a part of the working-class world he despises. Evie's ambiguous, shifting, and unplumbable significance is what makes *We Think the World of You* the only novel about gay desire that I've ever truly liked. It is the only novel I've read that truly conveys that desire's oscillations between identification and differentiation, between the fantasy of equality and the attractions of subordination.

Most novels and films about gay love and loss implicitly or explicitly propose that only when gay men are explicitly identified and represented can gay desire in an unequal world be triumphantly expressed. But Frank's struggles with Evie in his battle for Johnny's affection taught me something about the potential of a gay aesthetic grounded in the cardinal rule of not speaking its own name. Gay novels that equate gayness with its representation in an identity seem to exhaust the possibilities of a gay aesthetic with that act of singular representation. Paradoxical as it might sound, Evie can say more about gay desire by virtue of Frank saying less.

The novel also taught me that the aesthetic strategies required in a world of compulsory heterosexuality—the requirement to create an Evie as a diversion and a symbolic vessel for love—can tell the truth about the limitations of everyone's love. Millie says that just because her husband beats Evie, it doesn't mean he doesn't love her; after all, "he thinks the world of her, he do." "Just like your Johnny does of me!" Frank replies. What Frank wants from Evie—love on the terms of his world—is what everyone wants from Evie. So he reveals the truth, the grim and selfish truth, in the cliché that sounds throughout the novel. To conceive of our own desires—gay, straight, or otherwise—as the measure of the love others give us is not to be able to accept that love at all.

I almost feel guilty about extracting a meaning so moralizing out of a novel that uses humor to disturb all pieties of moral self-worth. Much of the novel's wit *appears* to be at the expense of the working class; Johnny's family's "low cunning . . . appeared to unite them in a silent conspiracy," and Megan "never seemed to have a grain of sense except where her own advantage was concerned." In the end, though, with Johnny returned to Megan and Evie finally given to Frank, his unwanted consolation prize, we discover whom the joke was on after all, as Frank realizes "that there was something in all this that I had missed." That someone like Frank can be the butt of one long and brutal joke is the ultimate victory of the humor of the gay aesthetic over the too-easy empathy demanded by gay identity. After all, who wants to build a world where you are forced to suffer another's pity instead of enjoying your own laughter?

Chapter Thirty-One

ALL AUNT HAGAR'S CHILDREN

EDWARD P. JONES

ELIZABETH GRAVER

MY CHILDHOOD drawings were not particularly skillful or original, but they were dense with people. I drew huge families (my own was small): brothers and sisters, mothers, fathers, grandparents all facing the viewer, each in a detailed outfit complete with hair ribbons, jewelry, and hats. At one point—I was maybe nine or ten—I developed an obsessive fear that without a set of ears, nostrils, tiny teeth, and ten fingers and toes, my figures would be deaf or suffocate or be unable to chew, open a school locker, or throw a ball. So I drew all the bits, clunkily but with a panicked sense of obligation. If the details came out particularly badly, I could always cover them—ears with hair, hands with an object or neighboring person. But they had to be there, underneath.

I thought of this recently when I reread Edward P. Jones's short-story collection *All Aunt Hagar's Children*. That book has taught me—for eventually I gave up drawing and became a fiction writer—an enormous amount about how to try to capture human complexity and give every character her due. My early efforts at fiction were sparsely populated, full of only children and isolated figures. I had a genuine interest in loneliness and inner life, but it is also just plain *hard* to do a lot of characters and not have them read as paper cutouts.

Jones's stories, though, are packed with people: male and female, old, young, and middle-aged: "They were the children of once-upon-a-time slaves, born into a kind of freedom, but they had traveled down through the wombs with what all their kind had been born with—the knowledge that God had promised next week to everyone but themselves." They are government workers and artists, veterans, convicts, doctors and shamans, schoolgirls, bureaucrats, porters. Many of them live in Washington, DC, having come up from the rural South as part of the Great Migration. If they are not related by blood, they are connected by a shared history of slavery, by common geographies, and by stories—from the Bible, folklore and fairy tale, neighborhood and communal life. Marked by pasts full of physical displacement, frayed or severed connections, and the legacies of state violence, they nonetheless keep expanding the definition of family by taking each other in.

Each of the fourteen stories here even has a "sibling" story in Jones's 1992 collection, *Lost in the City*. It's as if no story can stand in solitude but must link forward and back, inside and between the very pages of his books.

For a novel to be so richly peopled and communal would be less surprising—and indeed, Jones has written a prizewinning historical novel, *The Known World* (2003). But what he does with the perhaps more unforgiving form of the short story is astonishing, especially because the stories are also notable for their patient, delicate limning of interior life—loneliness, passion, boredom, sadness, even solitary mirth.

Take, for example, "Spanish in the Morning." It is, on the one hand, an utterly convincing portrait in the realist vein of a precocious little schoolgirl, as rich in psychological nuance as it is in tactile detail. The girl starts kindergarten on a wave of offerings—dresses, rulers, a pencil box—from her male relatives, for whom her education is a big deal. She makes a friend, jumps rope to playground chants ("I'm happy, you're happy / Go tell Mama, go tell Pappy"), witnesses an act of violence— two classmates getting slapped by the nuns because they are apparently boyfriend and girlfriend. She notices things: the hands on the clock, the back of a classmate's head, "the way the dark perfect skin of her neck flowed down from her yellow-ribboned hair, down, down beneath her collar. It was such a vulnerable neck."

On the other hand, the story breaks just about every writing workshop edict in its handling of point of view, narration, and the laws governing memory and time. Our first hint of this comes in the third paragraph: "I held my hands out for the money and thought of the first memory of my life—my grandfather playing little piggy on my toes when I was four weeks old." Come again? Four *weeks*? You *remember* that? So maybe the girl exaggerates for a moment, or her memory is supplemented by the stories she's been told. But then it keeps happening. This girl recalls so much, not just about her own infant memories but also about her parents' lives before her and about her grandfather's inner life. She even "remembers" that, years earlier, he lay near some train tracks in rural South Carolina, "dreaming that a child was sticking an especially long hatpin in his right leg as he weeded a section of his collard green patch in a cruel rain."

It soon becomes clear that this child narrator is part of a much bigger fabric, not just because she has a lot of relatives but also—and more radically—because she has access to her family's history of rupture and suffering. She somehow senses everything, down to the contours of their most private thoughts and the dogged ways that they have shaped their lives. "But this is about my father's father. And me. And all of them," she slips in at one point. Even the story's title, "Spanish in the Morning," has only an oblique relationship to the narrator. It refers not to her but to her mother, who has a thing for Spanish and speaks it in the morning, conversing "for long periods with some imaginary person, or conjugating verbs, staying sharp for the day that some woman from Mexico, lost and without a word of English, might knock on her door and ask for help."

Jones's ability to get at the inner lives of women is remarkable. He also manages to drop full histories into subordinate clauses, giving even side characters their due. "Then, in late August of 1899," he writes in "In the Blink of God's Eye," "Mrs. Halley Stafford, who, people said, had given her name to the comet, decided she had had enough and died in the bed she was conceived and born in." Mrs. Halley Stafford is not a central character. Yet now she has a story; in one sentence, we glimpse its comedy, its force, its cosmic arc.

Jones is not alone in his ability to tuck whole worlds inside the compact short-story form. Alice Munro does it beautifully. So do James Baldwin, William Faulkner, and (although often with a tighter focus) Grace Paley and Deborah Eisenberg. These are all writers who make bold use of time jumps and omniscient narration and for whom memory and the forces of history are central themes. But Jones's short stories deserve a wider audience than they have found. And at a time when so much of the news out of Washington, DC, comes to us in florescent-orange cartoon shapes, I am particularly grateful for his subtle rendering of the lives taking place in our capital's apartments and alleyways, transit buses and grocery stores, among the people who mop the floors of the government buildings and walk their children to the public schools.

Jones's stories remind us—so gently it is easy to overlook their underlying ferocity—that we are all just tiny figures inside the sweep of an often violent history. They offer songs, sermons, even sewing as ways to bear witness and forge connection. They make time buckle and blur the boundaries between self and other, dream and waking, the living and the dead. "The sounds of the other sleepers now came to her as well," Jones writes in the collection's final story, "Tapestry." "And there were many who were also talking in their sleep. Men and women shouting whole thoughts. A shout or two. A plea."

PART VI

MYSTERIES AND TRIALS

"**NOT ALL** books can be categorised within a genre, a plot, or a historical moment." Penny Fielding's description of feeling herself "inside a process without a predictable destination" when reading Graham Greene's *Stamboul Train* sums up what many of us enjoy feeling while immersed in a mystery. Margaret Cohen appreciates "the erroneous escapism" of the political thriller *Riddle of the Sands*. Yet she also sees Erskine Childers as "a writer fascinated by the ephemeral conditions occurring at the meeting of water and land—a zone of practical danger, keen nature knowledge, and poetry, all at once." Leah Price discovers in Celia Fremlin's *The Hours Before the Dawn* a new way of writing about motherhood: "If the agony of childbirth is epic, the discomfort that follows finds its natural home in the genre of the everynight . . . the mystery novel." Ramie Targoff, by contrast, shows that tucked inside the most seemingly formless of genres is clarity. The seventeenth-century diarist Anne Clifford reveals her single-minded devotion to that most *Law and Order* plot, an inheritance squabble: "What becomes clear, and oddly compelling, is the absolute lack of separation between her psyche and her estates."

Chapter Thirty-Two

THE DIARIES OF LADY ANNE CLIFFORD

RAMIE TARGOFF

MOVE OVER, Samuel Pepys. *The Diaries of Lady Anne Clifford* reveal the life of an extraordinary seventeenth-century woman who survived four monarchs, two husbands, one civil war, and a nearly forty-year legal battle before inheriting one of the greatest properties in England. Her first diary entry recounts the funeral of Elizabeth I in 1603, an event she watched from afar: at age thirteen, Clifford was not tall enough to walk as an official mourner alongside her mother, the countess of Cumberland, "which," she reported, "did much trouble me then." The last entry, in 1676, records the final weeks of her life, which she spent bedridden with illness.

In the seventy-three intervening years, Anne Clifford tracked nearly everything. We learn about her fights with her husband ("In the afternoon we again fell out"); her struggles with depression ("I stay'd at Home & was sad & melancholy"); her physical health ("All this week I kept to my chamber, because I found myself ill and weak"); her bodily functions ("I had seven or eight loose stools downwards"); her avid reading ("I sat and read much in the Turkish history and Chaucer"); her love of clothes ("I [tried] on my sea-water green satin gown"); her diet ("[I] ate so much cheese that it made me sick"); her lapses in religious practice ("I forgot it was fish day and ate flesh at both dinners"); her hobbies ("I wrought very hard and made an end of one of my cushions of Irish stitch work"); her leisure ("I spent most of the day in playing at tables"); her loneliness ("I am like an owl in the desert"). What emerges is a rich and complex portrait of a Renaissance woman for whom writing was not simply a habit but an essential part of her survival.

Clifford's earliest diary is known as the Knole Diary, named for the house she lived in with her first husband, Richard Sackville, earl of Dorset. It consists of one long memoir of 1603 and yearly entries for 1616–1619 that are broken down by month. Whatever records she kept from 1604–1615 have been lost. Clifford's central focus here is the often gripping story of her struggle to regain her family's lands after her father, George Clifford, third earl of Cumberland, disinherited her. Cumberland, one of the great privateers of the Elizabethan age, who became famous for his conquest of San Juan, Puerto Rico, had squandered away most of his money in gambling debts and poor investments. At the time of his death in 1605, he passed on both his debts and his properties to his brother, Sir Francis Clifford.

Clifford was an only child—her two brothers had died within a year of her birth—and ordinarily a daughter would not have expected to be her father's heir. But the Clifford estates in Westmorland and northwest Yorkshire, which covered nearly 90,000 acres, were subject to a special entail drawn up by Edward II in the early fourteenth century. That entail stipulated that the properties should descend to the direct heir without regard to sex. Within months of her father's death, Clifford and her mother filed the first of a series of lawsuits that Clifford would tirelessly fight for roughly the next forty years. The suit put her permanently at odds with her father's family: her uncle Francis and his son Henry became lifelong enemies. It also created horrible conflicts with her husband and her king, who pressured her to accept a substantial compensation in lieu of the inheritance (James offered her 17,000 pounds, roughly equivalent to two million pounds today). Clifford's refusal was met with cruel punishments: Dorset took away their young daughter, Margaret, for long stretches of time and regularly escaped to one of his family homes with his secretary, Matthew Caldicott. When Dorset was with Clifford, he turned down her invitations to sleep with her in her bedroom (despite his bad behavior, she remained oddly fond of him). Clifford recorded all of this without any sign of embarrassment or shame, treating her diary as her most intimate friend.

The diaries Clifford kept between 1620 and 1649 have not survived outside of occasional passages that were copied elsewhere. These entries, incorporated into a biographical narrative, are included in a middle section of this book entitled, "The Years Between." For our purposes, her diaries resume in 1650, when her position dramatically changed: following her cousin Francis's death in 1643 and without a male heir, Clifford finally inherited all of her father's estates. At this point, her writing takes on a very different tone. In place of the richly described emotional turmoil of her marriage to Dorset and her lawsuit, the diaries now become a somewhat obsessive register of her life as high sheriffess of Westmorland.

What becomes clear, and oddly compelling, is the absolute lack of separation between her psyche and her estates. Clifford describes in numbing detail, for example, the repairs made to her properties: "I caused my mill about a mile from Barden Tower . . . to be pulled down and new built up again with stone and wood at my own charge"; "I caused a great part of Appleby Church to be taken down (it being very ruinous and in danger of falling of itself)"; "By my directions was also my decayed Castle of Pendragon in Mallerstang . . . begun to be repaired, which had lain waste . . . ever since the time of King Edward III." But she also narrates events in the larger world that are oddly refracted through the lens of her particular location. King James's daughter, Elizabeth, queen of Bohemia, died while "I now lying in Brougham Castle in Westmoreland." The fire of London, which raged through the city in the summer of 1666 and left most of it in ruins, took place while "my Daughter of Thanet and her three youngest Daughters lay here in Skipton Castle with me." News of her own family was treated in the same vein: a great-granddaughter was born while "I [was] lying now in my house or castle of Skipton in Craven." Her daughter Isabella died while "I [did] lie in my own chamber in Appleby Castle," although, she added, she did not hear of the death until she moved to Pendragon Castle, "where I now lay in the second story that looks east and south."

Accounting details worthy of *Moll Flanders* are likewise jumbled up with memories of events from her distant past. The last entries she made in her diary before her death in March 1676 include minute records of household purchases: she pays back a servant for the purchase of 249 yards of linen cloth bought to make sheets and pillowcases; she agrees to buy five dozen yards of lace. She also notes, two days before dying, that it was the sixtieth anniversary of the day she and her mother, visiting the same castle where Clifford lay in bed, informed the courts they would not take King James's offer. This decision, she observed, "did spin out a great deal of trouble to us, yet God turned it for the best."

The final entry in Clifford's diary is the only one written by someone else. "On Wednesday the 22nd, about 6 a clock in the afternoon," it begins, "in her own chamber in Brougham Castle wherein her noble father was born and her blessed mother died, [she] yielded up her precious soul." According to the anonymous writer, Clifford's last words were: "I thank God I am very well." Her corpse was placed in her coach and driven to St. Lawrence Church in Appleby, where she was buried next to her mother. Her friend Edward Rainbow, bishop of Carlisle, delivered the funeral sermon on Proverbs 14.1: "Every wise woman buildeth her house." The biblical verse had certainly met its match.

THE RIDDLE
OF THE SANDS

Erskine Childers

No. 29 in the Mariners Library

Chapter Thirty-Three

THE RIDDLE OF THE SANDS

ERSKINE CHILDERS

MARGARET COHEN

EVER SINCE James Cook nearly wrecked his ship on the Great Barrier Reef in 1770, European publics have turned to South Sea cays and atolls when they craved adventures in the shallows. This environmental Orientalism has left the drab, sulfurous North Atlantic marshes and mudflats a distant, dismal-seeming second. Yet intertidal lowlands also make rich artistic terrain. Perhaps the most tantalizing and lyrical exploration of those desolate spaces was penned by Erskine Childers, a British civil servant and soldier whose intensifying engagement with Irish nationalism led to his execution in 1922.

His only novel, *The Riddle of the Sands: A Record of Secret Service*, originally published in 1903, is a top-drawer spy adventure. Yet it is also the travelogue of a bourgeois vacation gone terribly awry. And in sharp contrast to later examples of the genre (Thomas Mann's *Death in Venice*, Paul Bowles's *The Sheltering Sky*), its tale of erroneous escapism devolves not into existential crisis but into global political intrigue.

The novel begins when a slightly Dr. Watson–like young Englishman, Carruthers, is invited on a duck hunt by Davies, an obscure Oxford acquaintance. Of their destination, the sand banks and shallows of the Wadden Sea (that is, the Frisian Islands and the intertidal areas of the North Sea off Denmark, Holland, and Germany), Carruthers at first has nothing more to say than, "They look rather desolate." He has to replace his fantasies of relaxing on "orderly, snowy decks and basket chairs under the awning aft" with the reality of "roughing it in a shabby little yacht, utterly out of my element," with a companion who seems "a tiresome enigma."

As Davies initiates Carruthers into the Wadden Sea's tortuous channels and tidal shallows, Carruthers begins to realize they are tracking momentous quarry. Why was Davies's kedge, the *Dulcibella*, almost lured to destruction upon the East Hohenhörn sands? Davies comes to suspect that the mysterious Herr Dollmann, who had led him astray, is an Englishman turned German spy. At the novel's beginning, Carruthers casually mentions he spent time in France and Germany following studies at Oxford; lo and behold, Davies has invited him along precisely because of the knowledge acquired on that German sojourn.

In a chase after Dollmann, Carruthers and Davies feel their way through what Carruthers first calls a "desert of sand," where, Davies exalts, "you can explore for days without seeing a soul." The novel includes factual sea charts to orient readers in the labyrinth of intertidal flats, marshes, and dunes that the protagonists crisscross over the novel's chapters. One of them is marked with a fictional location: where the *Dulcibella* was stranded, shown in figure 33.2.

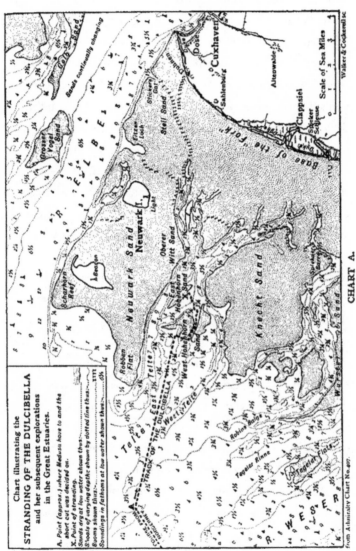

CHART A.

The charts certainly orient the characters' convoluted navigations; however, their importance as a plot guide soon falls away. What matters far more is the conviction that the sands abstracted on the charts are an opportunity for entrancing description and narrative enigma, worthy of readerly note. Like Mark Twain's *Life on the Mississippi*, *The Riddle of the Sands* was penned by a writer fascinated by the ephemeral conditions occurring at the meeting of water and land—a zone of practical danger, keen nature knowledge, and poetry, all at once.

The hunt to find Dollmann and to discover his motives is no more important to the novel's allure than the picture Childers paints of this intoxicatingly mutable sandscape. In place of a sterile desert, Carruthers begins to perceive colors that "varied from light fawn, where the highest levels had dried in the wind, to brown or deep violet, where it was still wet, and slate-grey where patches of mud soiled its clean bosom. Here and there were pools of water, smitten into ripples by the impotent wind; here and there it was speckled by shells and seaweed." The nuances of the ebbing and flooding tide are enhanced by the mystery of the capricious, shifting autumnal fogs. Sometimes the "fog" is "silent, clammy, nothing visible." At other times it shrouds the landscape in a ghostly mood. When "a blanket of white fog" rolls in and Carruthers must guide Davies back "with a foghorn," the device's "music roused hosts of sea birds from the surrounding flats and brought them wheeling and complaining round us, a weird invisible chorus to my mournful solo."

The enigma unraveled in *The Riddle of the Sands* is tucked away in "a quantity of insignificant streams and tidal outlets."

There the German navy is hard at work building an "armada" of barges "capable of flinging themselves on a correspondingly obscure and therefore unexpected portion of" Britain's coast. At the novel's climax, Carruthers inadvertently participates in a rehearsal for this invasion when he stows away on one such German vessel. A naval arms race between Britain and Germany was in fact occurring as Childers wrote *The Riddle of the Sands*. Its author believed what the American Alfred Thayer Mahan asserted in *The Influence of Sea Power Upon History, 1660–1783* (1890): who controls the seas, controls the globe. As Davies puts it, Germany is "our great trade rival of the present, our great naval rival of the future . . . an ever more formidable factor in the future of our delicate network of empire."

English readers hearkened to the novel's call to arms. Legend has it that Winston Churchill gave the book credit for spurring the Admiralty to build naval bases on the North Sea, such as at Scapa Flow in the Orkney Islands, in 1904. The importance of the North Sea in Britain's two subsequent wars with Germany is history. When looking for a place to hide during the stowaway episode, Carruthers remarks pointedly on the absence of an apple-barrel such as used by Jim in *Treasure Island*. Lest his tale of littoral sleuthing be relegated to adventure storybook, Childers underscores the world-historical importance of his novel's tussles in the shallows.

Davies and Carruthers fear national invasion; today, however, simmering international conflict recalls Childers's insistence on the geopolitical consequence of seemingly insignificant shoals and sands. The current Spratly Island dispute in the South China Sea, for example, was inflamed when China started building up remote reefs into islands, starting in 2013. With maritime features transformed into land, China is extending territorial claims over one of the most commercially valuable waterways of the globe, where trillions of dollars of freight pass every year. The dispute continues to escalate, implicating mercantile transport and involving Vietnam, the Philippines, Taiwan, and Malaysia, as well as other global sea powers like the United States, although it does not often make our front-page news.

The Riddle of the Sands also accrues new meaning in the Anthropocene era. Childers created his fictional world from a resource now rapidly disappearing because of the building boom around the world, in one of the present moment's least discussed ecological depletions.[1] Concrete requires sea sand— desert sand is too fine for such use. As a recent *Economist* article notes, sand dredging "causes pollution and harms local biodiversity. Thinning coastlines affect beaches' capacity to absorb stormy weather."[2]

A maxim of activism is that to care about an issue, people must be able to connect to it emotionally. As *The Riddle of the Sands* brings to granular life the environment of Davies and Carruthers' treacherous navigations, it may draw the attention of today's readers to a precious—and fragile—planetary resource.

NOTES

1. See Vince Beiser, *The World in a Grain of Sand: The Story of Sand and How It Transformed Civilization* (New York: Riverhead, 2018).
2. R. S., "Why There Is a Shortage of Sand," *The Economist*, April 24, 2017.

Chapter Thirty-Four

STAMBOUL TRAIN

GRAHAM GREENE

PENNY FIELDING

GRAHAM GREENE'S 1932 novel *Stamboul Train* concludes with two of the train's passengers visiting a musical show in Istanbul, the end of the line. A third passenger has traveled on the train to perform in the show. Although the two in the audience don't know it yet, the third passenger won't be appearing onstage because she has just died of a heart attack. The chorus members blow whistles and sing:

> Waiting at the station
> For a near relation
> Puff, puff, puff, puff—

The song fragments seem to disappear with the engine in a puff of smoke. What exactly is "a near relation"—a close relative or a close encounter? Perhaps a lover, but in any case something narrowly missed, two things that don't quite coincide, a relation that can't be properly measured or compared. The novel's ending leaves ambiguous whether the two people listening to the song will form a union, and the third has missed her appointment to appear in the show. We readers, too, are left—even at the terminus—waiting and hoping.

In Graham Greene's famous later novels, his protagonists struggle with substantial questions of responsibility, duty, and action. *The Heart of the Matter* (1948) traces a conflict between religious faith and secular love. *The Quiet American* (1956) acutely forecasts how blind American righteousness and European world-weariness would, in tandem, devastate Vietnam. However, his second novel, *Stamboul Train*, never develops such well-wrought abstractions. It is structured by missed opportunities, relationships broken off or uncompleted and unfulfilled political aspirations. Individual characters seem caught up in historical change, but that history appears uncertain and difficult for readers to process, even with the benefit of hindsight.

Looking back from our own (equally gloomy) day, the dire events of the 1930s loom large: the novel is punctuated by casual and vicious anti-Semitism, and Hitler became chancellor of Germany the year after the book appeared. We're pulled between that terrible future and the novel's own present, between dreadful foreboding and the frustration of the characters' inability to act decisively in their own time. It's as if Greene has inserted these looming portents into a history that is still unformed yet beginning to take shape.

All that may sound as maddening as the enigma of the "near relation," yet this early novel was his reputation maker, and for good reason. In the first few pages of *Stamboul Train* we meet Dr. Richard John (seemingly a Briton)—only to discover that he is in fact the Serbian revolutionary leader Richard Czinner. As the train pulls out of Ostend station, Czinner thinks about the reasons for his own journey and tries to insert his own sense of purpose into some form of historical narrative: "If I could sleep, he thought with longing, I could remember more clearly the things that have to be remembered."

Czinner is the closest the novel comes to a clarifying protagonist, the sort who might clearly mark the novel as a political thriller representing a clearly demarcated struggle for national freedom. His memories of his past as a revolutionary leader, though, shed no light on the present political situation. The uprising he is traveling to join starts without him, and he finds himself stranded in a historical stream that he can't directly experience: "They had left him in an empty house which could not find a tenant because old ghosts were sometime vocal in the rooms, and Dr. Czinner himself now was not even the latest ghost." In the novel's strange temporality, Czinner is doubly out of time; his history has become a house haunted by its past, but that history has no clear future.

As the train moves on, Greene delineates a series of characters struggling to gain or elucidate a purpose in their lives. Looking back on the novel in his 1971 autobiography, Greene wrote: "By the time I finished *Stamboul Train*, the *days of security* had almost run out." His primary meaning here is that his financial security was precarious and he needed to make money from the novel. *Stamboul Train*, though, undermines the notion of security in all sorts of forms, including its own status as an "entertainment" or thriller.

Greene did make money from the novel: in 1934, it was even made into a movie called (like the novel when it appeared in the United States) *Orient Express*. One result is that when Agatha Christie's *Murder on the Orient Express* was published, also in 1934, its U.S. title was *Murder on the Calais Coach*. Yet it's worth noting how different Christie's brilliantly generic plot is from Greene's. In Christie's *Murder on the Orient Express*, the plot comes to a doubly satisfying conclusion, when Poirot assembles all the suspects in the dining car and reveals the culprit . . . They all did it! Rather than face any awkward legal ramifications, however, Christie gives the characters a moral, extralegal justification. The killing was in revenge for a child murder, and Poirot airily decides not to inform the police and to let the killers leave the train. The big reveal in *Murder on the Orient Express* is that the seemingly random characters are all there for a shared secret purpose.

In *Stamboul Train*, partnerships, alliances, and hostilities form and reform; there are no shared motives, only "near relations." Cast adrift from acting with either historical or generic functions, the characters move through the novel, enacting moments of experience that can't be fully assimilated into the conventions of a thriller or a political novel or a whodunit. For instance: instead of a death acting as a key plot function, as crime thrillers demand, Greene's novel focuses on the experience of what it would be like to die; *Stamboul Train* includes two scenes imagining this moment. Nor do characters come together in everyday ways. Voices become disembodied: a whole section reproduces snatches of conversation on the train without the speakers being clearly identified. The visual field, too, is blurred or even surreal: "faces streamed away," "a tender light flooded the compartment . . . human beings floated liked goldfish."

These moments evade explanation. The novel is interested in sleep and records the dreams of many of its characters, but it explicitly rejects psychoanalysis as a way of explaining them, however much Czinner longs for sleep as a point of access to memory. Psychoanalysis takes place in the present, but it is also a retrospective process that retells a story and so gives it order and legibility. These are satisfactions that *Stamboul Train* never delivers. We readers are never with Poirot in the restaurant car, putting motives and actions together in sequence. Nor are we with Freud in the consulting room, making a coherent narrative out of dream images.

Stamboul Train takes its place among other twentieth-century novels in which espionage and wartime secrecy are glimpsed through a lens that obscures motives and renders people uncanny. Set in London during the Blitz, Elizabeth Bowen's *The Heat of the Day* (1948) evokes the same strange, haunted atmosphere that surrounds Greene's Richard Czinner. The novel's main characters—all involved in secret intelligence—appear to each other as shadowy, ultimately indecipherable figures. When Stella looks at her lover Robert (who is passing secrets to the Germans), she notices how "in the unfamiliar, the familiar persisted like a ghost." Muriel Spark's *The Hothouse by the East River* (1973) takes this a step further: its wartime spies, now living in New York, turn out to be actual ghosts.

Like those distant cousins, Greene's *Stamboul Train* captures the temporality of experience. We feel things happening in the present, but that present is haunted by an incomplete understanding of history and an anxious apprehension of the future. Not all books can be categorized within genres or all plots within specific historical moments. *Stamboul Train* is a reminder of this. Reading it, I find myself inside a process without a predictable destination.

The HOURS BEFORE DAWN

A NOVEL BY
CELIA FREMLIN

Chapter Thirty-Five

THE HOURS BEFORE DAWN

CELIA FREMLIN

LEAH PRICE

AS CELIA Fremlin told it three decades after the fact, *The Hours Before Dawn* was written at night. Lurching around Hampstead Heath behind a stroller that she was barely awake enough to maneuver, Fremlin realized that parental sleeplessness "is a major human experience." "Why hasn't someone written about it?" she wondered. "It seemed to me that a serious novel should be written with this experience at its centre. Then it occurred to me—why don't I write one?"

The rhetorical question isn't unanswerable. If there's anyone less articulate than an infant, it's a groggy adult. But Fremlin saw, through her own postpartum fog, the literary potential of that cognitive impairment. If the agony of childbirth is epic, the discomfort that follows finds its natural home in the genre of the everynight, the novel. More specifically, the mystery novel. New parents are ready-made for noir. They creep around like burglars trying to find a diaper without switching on the light; they edge a bottle out of a sleeping mouth with the dexterity of a pickpocket. Well-restedness may be a precondition of reliability, but unreliable narrators have their charms.

The Hours Before Dawn, Fremlin's first novel, is focalized through the bleary eyes of a new mother, Louise, whose stroller seems to vanish and reappear at unpredictable moments of the night. (If you don't want a spoiler, put down this article until you've gotten your hands on the book, recently republished in both the United States and the UK). "Seems," because we hardly know whom to believe, Louise or her better-rested husband. Or perhaps their spinster lodger, whose hidden diary eventually reveals her refusal to believe that her own pregnancy miscarried.

Fremlin's reputation today, such as it is, rests more on her account of stumbling into postpartum authorship than on any of the sixteen novels that followed. Like the Everymom anecdotes retailed by today's baby bloggers, though, Fremlin's blurring of the lines between fiction and autobiography understates her professional capital. Until marriage, Fremlin had followed a familiar path for leftists of both genders in the years between the wars. A communist at Oxford, she broke into print with an exposé based on her stint as a cleaning lady. She went on to become one of the earliest recruits to Mass-Observation, a project that enlisted up to sixty volunteers at a time to eavesdrop in pubs, lodging houses, and, later, air-raid shelters and munitions factories.

Her characters watch one another to more sinister effect. Like some Mass-Observer gone rogue, the bereaved lodger in *Hours* scours surrounding households for babies who might be hers, getting a foot in their doors by posing variously as "the lady from the Welfare; and the lady about the milk vouchers; and the lady about Em's special boots . . . the lady about the Registrations, and the lady from the School Attendance." Closer to home, Louise scans her child's face for twitches that might hint at impending sleepiness, while the lodger parses the color of the same infant's hair for a clue that he might be her stolen son.

Zenith Radio Corporation's 1937 "Radio Nurse"—what would later come to be called the baby monitor—brought surveillance into family homes three decades before CCTV. Fremlin's characters act, at times, like human nanny cams. A former classics student, Fremlin may have intended the mothers whom she dubbed "the cat race" to function as a chorus. Jane Austen would have called them a neighborhood of voluntary spies.

The neighborhood in question is Hampstead Garden Suburb, a planned development just north of Fremlin's own more bohemian home. As well as banning pubs, its founders forbade garden walls: hedges provided a more convenient barrier for neighbors to spy though. Like the landlady-lodger dyad, though, the relations among neighbors fascinated Fremlin. She noticed, for example, that it was considered as rude to knock before entering the other half of a semi as *not* to knock when entering an adjacent single-family house.

Fremlin's original back-flap bio chirped that "she finds the running of a house and the writing of novels an ideal combination of jobs, as . . . neither demands a rigid adherence to set hours." At three in the morning, though, set hours start to look underrated. In what were coming to be known as "bed-room suburbs," wives took the night shift while husbands slept: the suburbs segregated the sexes not just in space but in time.

Fremlin's training for a second-class circadian status came as an air-raid warden, but the Battle of Britain turned out to be nothing compared to a colicky daughter. When Louise, desperate to remove the crying baby from earshot so that her husband can sleep enough to wake in time to catch the next morning's commuter train, trundles the stroller off to the playground at midnight, she reclaims for women the same right that men enjoy: to work outside the home. She ends up being escorted home by a policeman.

What does Fremlin have to offer U.S. readers? Think of her as the lovechild of C. Wright Mills (personal experience generalized into "sociological imagination") and Shirley Jackson (dark humor limning maternal misery). *The Hours Before Dawn* might be an ancestor to the 1992 U.S. box-office blockbuster *The Hand That Rocks the Cradle*, the main difference being that as the scene shifts from postwar London to post–Cold War Washington, the lodger becomes a live-in nanny. Where Fremlin's novel looks forward to the surveillance of the welfare state, Curtis Hanson's film embroiders on an ancien regime fear of the wet nurse, showing Rebecca de Mornay's clock alarm beeping at three a.m., when it's time for her to sneak into the baby's room and unbutton her nightgown. Fremlin, always matter-of-fact, would have known that the hours before dawn are the worst possible time to tiptoe around the parents of a baby.

Yet the closest equivalent to Fremlin's patch of North London may be the canyon housing developments of Southern California. Those were chronicled by the noir novelist Margaret Millar, as great as Fremlin and as inexplicably forgotten. Millar shared Fremlin's insight that the novel could skewer suburban gender relations more nimbly than could essayistic satires like Friedan's 1963 *The Feminine Mystique*.

Millar too zeroed in on women keeping watch through the picture window over the open-plan sink. *A Stranger in My Grave* (1960), for instance, aims to reconstruct what happened in her own life on a particular day—December 2, 1955—that remains a blank in her memory. Where realists of Henry James's generation substituted irritation for rage as their characters' dominant emotion, Millar and Fremlin make scatterbrained forgetfulness do the work accomplished in gothic fiction by concussion-induced amnesia. Fremlin's con artists get away with murder because their victims distrust their own memories after a bad night's sleep.

Now that Hampstead is being bought up by Russian plutocrats, the not-yet-cool Britannia of *The Hours Before Dawn* may feel distant. Postwar housing shortages generated lodgers, postwar real-estate speculation generated bedroom suburbs, and postwar social welfare generates an alibi for a psychopath who wants to pose as an orthopedic visiting nurse. Yet Fremlin's domestic gothic comes out of a more durable tradition. *Uncle Paul* (1959) is only her most explicit riff on *Northanger Abbey*—the main update being to replace Austen's Bath with an off-season RV park.

Fremlin's turf centers on what Henry James called "those most mysterious of mysteries, the mysteries which are at our own doors." James was referring to Victorian sensation novelist Mary Elizabeth Braddon, whose plots hinge on sex, whether in the form of seduction or more decorous bigamy. Fremlin's characters, though, aren't jumping into bed with anyone; they rarely make it into bed at all. After some red herrings hint that the lodger might hanker after Louise's husband, the final plot twist reveals the real tug-of-war to be over Louise's baby. In a space devoid of men during the workday, the Victorian courtship plot gives way to plots of motherhood.

Make that landladyhood, for in recasting Bluebeard's chamber as a bedsit, Fremlin changes the unit of narrative interest from a family—whether husband or baby—to a household. *Hours* opens with a neighbor warning Louise to think carefully about making up for her lost wages by renting out a room. It turns out to be good advice, though at the time the neighbor's grounds for worrying sound lurid: she knows a landlady whose lodgers moved in with a suspiciously heavy parcel, then flitted, leaving behind their imbecile sister.

By the end of *Hours* (spoiler alert again), the lodger has walked off with Louise's baby. Perhaps the most frightening thing about its plot is the spectacle of an older economy in which crime serves to avoid caretaking responsibilities— hiding your disabled sister in a cardboard box or, more classically, drowning your baby in the pond—being replaced by a low-birth-rate welfare state in which the need to be needed drives crime.

In a later novel, *Possession*, from 1969, Fremlin depicts an overprotective mother who inspires in more permissive mothers "the same flush of pitying scorn that virtuous women used to feel on coming into contact with prostitutes." Since that time, the replacement of husband by baby has become nigh-on complete. So far, how-to books and satire are the main genres to have emerged from American attachment parenting. One wonders what new novelistic forms will eventually do justice to the dark nights of its practitioners' souls.

PART VII

JOURNEYS OF THE SPIRIT

FIRST, THERE is the sheer joy of the trip. "Few poets seem to have more fun than Patience Agbabi" writes Stephanie Burt about the shapeshifting poetic energy of Patience Agbabi's *Transformatrix*. Vanessa Smith loves that there is "something Zen" in *A Life of One's Own*, but she also delights in "lively hedonism" that Marion Milner chronicles: her experiments with "new dances and clothes, jazz clubs and ping-pong, sleeping under the stars and nude sunbathing." The sculptor Joe Brainard, in *I Remember*, makes word collages out of everything from rocks and wine to fold-out trays: Andrew Miller concludes that "part of the pleasure comes from listening for the harmonics of the thing, the way that the memories work together and apart, never giving you everything but always giving you something."

Underneath that joy, something more serious can also be afoot. John Williams's *Butcher's Crossing* seduces readers into gazing down into a deadly but awe-inspiring river, "a deep but transparent greenish brown, . . . flow[ing] past in thick ropes and sheeted wedges, in shapes that changed with an incredible complexity before his gaze." And Theo Davis's celebration of Satomi Myodo (who disarmingly explains "I wanted to know why I was such bad wood") sums up the book's greatness in her unforgettable opening line: "As spiritual autobiographies go, *Journey in Search of the Way* is a bit of a romp."

Chapter Thirty-Six

A LIFE OF ONE'S OWN

MARION MILNER

VANESSA SMITH

I RARELY fail to remember my first encounter with a book—it usually becomes merged with the story of the book—so it is disconcerting to me to realize that I have no recollection of how I first latched onto Marion Milner's *A Life of One's Own* (1934). Someone must have told me to read it, or it could have cropped up in a footnote. This forgetting feels different from an ordinary lapse of memory, more vehement—my mind refuses to go there. *A Life of One's Own* has always felt as though it were waiting just for me: a thinking person's self-help book. In it, Milner sets herself an apparently simple task: to attend to the daily meanderings of mood, with the particular aim of tracking her own happiness. There is something about Milner's appeal to the possibility of experiencing something of "one's own" that invites one to reject any sense of indebtedness to the forgotten source, to feel directly addressed.

As powerful as this sense of universality, though, is the book's historical specificity. *A Life* offers unprecedentedly direct access to the mind and feelings of an early twentieth-century educated working woman. Marion Blackett was twenty-six when she began the research for the book, in 1926, and thirty-four when she published it, under the pseudonym Joanna Field. She had completed a degree in psychology and physiology, in 1923, and soon after started working for the National Institute of Industrial Psychology, headed by Charles Samuel Myers, collecting data from various factories and industrial workplaces across England. The winter of 1927–28 was spent in the United States on a Rockefeller scholarship, attending Elton Mayo's seminars at Harvard Business School.

She had married Dennis Milner just before leaving for the States; their son, John, was born in 1932. Dennis's chronic illness meant that Marion had to return immediately to work: she taught psychology to the Workers' Educational Association in the East End of London and also undertook research for the Girls' Public Day School Trust (published in 1938 as *The Human Problem in Schools*). She would eventually begin training with the British Psychoanalytical Society, in 1940, and later practiced as a psychoanalyst for many years, but *A Life of One's Own* and Milner's second book, *An Experiment in Leisure* (1937), sit emphatically outside the psychoanalytic canon.

Milner's beef with psychoanalysis is not with the premise that our impulses are intricately complex but with the idea that expertise outside the self is required to track them. "The psycho-analysts," she writes, "had always given me the feeling that they considered the unconscious mind as a sort of special preserve which no layman must tamper with." In beginning to reclaim this preserve for the lay self, Milner starts writing regular diary entries:

> I began on a Sunday. This was the only day when I had leisure enough to catch up with the smaller necessities of my life, darning, writing letters, general tidying-up. By the end of the day all I could find to say in my diary was: "Rather oppressed with the number of things to be done." The only special happiness that I could remember was hearing someone playing the piano in the distance and watching the splashing water in my bath. The next day, back at my work, I apparently had only one moment which seemed important. It was a moment of absent-mindedness when I looked up from my desk and found myself gazing at grey roofs and chimneys, a view typical from a million of London's top-floor windows. I do not remember what I saw but only the shock of delight in just looking.

While this exercise, which she terms "a kind of preliminary mental account-keeping," may come across as a subtle comment on the unquantifiability of the value in female labor, its appeal for me lies less in its recording of quotidian charms than in its broader recognition of the rewards of abstractedness.

As her experiment progresses, Milner follows the body rather than thought, observation rather than will. In activities from simple game playing to drawing and singing, she gains access to a new level of awareness and skill, finding that "if I used my will to keep my attention fixed on the end I wanted to achieve and on keeping my muscles relaxed, then the body knew how to find its own means, I did not have to think about what my limbs were doing at all."

She sketches well when she sketches in haste, trying to capture the thing rather than playing the careful artist; she sings in tune when she catches herself unawares. She observes more effectively when she doesn't drive her sensations: "I was finding that my eye had quite definite interests of its own, that when it was not driven into being the slave of my desires, or browbeaten into providing me with information, it liked looking at things for their own sake and saw quite a different world."

While this may sound Zen, there is a lively hedonism to her search for sources of enjoyment. She tries new dances and clothes, jazz clubs and ping-pong, sleeping under the stars and nude sunbathing. The book also explores manifestations of boredom, anxiety, and hatred, but her focus on positive affect aligns *A Life of One's Own* with a broader interwar commitment to the upbeat—today we party, for who knows what lies ahead. Others in Britain were conducting similar experiments: Bertrand Russell's *The Conquest of Happiness* was published in 1930; Mass-Observation ran a competition in Bolton in 1938 asking respondents to rank ten "qualities of life." Milner similarly resorts to lists at various points in her book, mentioning, under "Things I love": "the abandon and moods of dogs," "fairs, loitering in a crowd," "old implements," and "people singing out of doors."

Milner draws upon kinds of evidence that are part and parcel of the "mindfulness" syllabus: journal writing, meditation and breathing exercises, dream transcription, free-associative writing, automatic drawing. However, as a trained social scientist, she frames her approach methodically. By offering hypotheses, tests, and controls, she subtly reconfigures leisure and pleasure as forms of work. At the same time, she rethinks work practices, including her own writing, in ways that resonate with dynamics of play. She rejects striving and narrow focus in favor of receptivity, pleasure, and creative license.

This disjunction between approach and subject matter is the secret of the book's enduring appeal. In *A Life*, all the perverse delight of snooping in a private journal is nested within a philosophically strenuous reading experience. Milner gets her readers to rethink the separation of spheres of work and leisure: to find imaginative possibility in daily tasks and to be more thoughtful and practice-based in using our down time.

In the process, she unostentatiously offers a prescient and highly original account of subjectivity, by taking the self as estranged object and treating personal feeling as matter for observation. Like the analyst she proves she can do without, she provides a method of noticing patterns of response and so of freeing ourselves from their sway. Like the modernist novelist she almost is, she invites us to retrieve the familiar from a stream of consciousness yet to bring self-reflection to our drive for identification. The "own" life is every reader's prerogative.

Chapter Thirty-Seven

BUTCHER'S CROSSING

JOHN WILLIAMS

JOHN PLOTZ

CANYONLANDS NATIONAL Park, Utah, 103°F under a cloudless summer sky. I'd call the canyon floor below "bone-white," if it looked like anything had ever lived there long enough to leave its bones behind. This is the part of the world where Edward Abbey (in his 1968 *Desert Solitaire*) said he came "to look at and into a juniper tree, a piece of quartz, a vulture, a spider, and see it as in itself, devoid of all humanly ascribed qualities, anti-Kantian." And something like what Thoreau had in mind when he talked about "Earth . . . made out of Chaos and Old Night . . . no man's garden, but the unhandselled globe."

If you'd told me a month earlier that when I reached southern Utah humanity would soon start feeling like an irrelevancy—even a kind of irreverence—I would barely have looked up from my latte and iPhone long enough to chuckle. Still, it happened. I had a glimpse of "Matter, vast, terrific"

(Thoreau again) and a sense of what a juniper tree or a piece of quartz might be up to . . . without me. I don't know if the feeling was anti-Kantian, but it sure was memorable.

Yet as I struggled with the arid skeleton-scape of Canyonlands, my best guidance came from a book deeply skeptical about the redemptive power of that kind of inhuman emptiness. The way John Williams's *Butcher's Crossing* (1960) tells it, the idea of embracing Nature's inhumanity is not only naive, it's downright destructive. Thoreau's dreams of "Contact! Contact!" do not *solve* humanity's rapacious relationship with Nature—they are simply another incarnation of that rapacity. An opening epigraph from Melville sets the novel's uneasy, almost sinister tone: "Aye, and poets send out the sick spirits to green pasture, like lame horses. . . . Poets have it that for sore hearts . . . nature is the grand cure. But who froze to death my teamster on the prairie?"

Critics have singled out movies of the early 1970s (*Butch Cassidy and the Sundance Kid, The Outlaw Josey Wales, McCabe and Mrs. Miller, Jeremiah Johnson*) and some novels of the early 1980s (especially Cormac McCarthy's *Blood Meridian*) as the first wave of "revisionist westerns." But back in 1960, without McCarthy's lurid baroque extravagances, without any cool Hollywood soundtrack, John Williams wrote what may be the perfect *anti*-western. *Butcher's Crossing* is a novel that turns upside down the expectations of the genre—and goes to war with a century of American triumphalism, a century of regeneration through violence, a century of senseless slaughter. To say it's an attack on Eisenhower's America is right enough; only we shouldn't be so sure that it doesn't also apply to

Kennedy's New Frontier and to a half-century of triumphalism and exceptionalism since, under Republicans and Democrats alike.

In recent years scholars and readers have rediscovered *Stoner*, John Williams's 1965 campus novel about a farmer's boy turned unhappy and ultimately unsuccessful professor. Its Hollywood pitch might be "*Jude the Obscure* meets *The Professor's House*"—can't you hear producers rushing to acquire the rights? About Williams's 1948 first novel, *Nothing but the Night*, the only good thing to be said is that he quickly disowned it. Williams's austere, meditative *Augustus* (a National Book Award winner in 1973) may not rival Marguerite Yourcenar's *Memoirs of Hadrian*, but it offers a very touching portrait of ancient Stoicism, a doomed but admirable effort to preserve one's private dignity in the face of public horror.

Butcher's Crossing is in a different league from these other works. The novel is about a buffalo hunt in the late 1870s, just before the coming of the trains finished carving up buffalo country and the European market for buffalo robes collapsed: the bursting of the Buffalo Bubble. The novel chronicles a hunting party that heads out from Butcher's Crossing, Kansas, into the Front Range of the Rockies. They're searching for a valley hunters haven't yet emptied of its buffalo herd—one of those herds that stretches far as the eye can see. The wealthy Bostonian Will Andrews, an Emerson- and Thoreau-quoting preacher's son, hires the hardened mountain man Miller and a pair of his old-school associates (a skinner and a cook) in the novel's first part. The second and longest part follows the hunt;

the third details its miserable aftermath back at Butcher's Crossing.

Early on, Miller comes across as positively satanic. The one appearance Native Americans make in the novel is in a remark he tosses off en route to the killing valley: "River Indians . . . they ain't worth shooting anymore." When Andrews witnesses Miller becoming a killing machine, no reader can doubt where the true evil resides:

> During the last hour of the stand he came to see Miller as a mechanism, an automaton, moved by the moving herd; and he came to see Miller's destruction of the buffalo, not as a lust for blood or a lust for the hides or a lust for what the hides would bring, or even at last the blind lust of fury that toiled darkly within him—he came to see the destruction as a cold, mindless response to the life in which Miller had immersed himself.

In an idyllic valley tucked between towering peaks, straight out of Zane Grey, Miller mills buffaloes into salable piles of hides.

We know how to read this: a clash between young civility and bloodthirsty evil. In *Heart of Darkness* terms, Andrews is the novel's Marlow, its callow, suffering storyteller, and Miller its demoniacal Kurtz. Yet Andrews bought the guns, the wagons, even the lead they melt for Miller's bullets.

So what does Williams want his readers to make of Andrews's Emersonian optimism and Miller's pragmatic murderousness?

After the failure of the hunt, Andrews and Miller come back home to meet the embittered hides dealer McDonald, who has been bankrupted by shifting fashions back in Europe and is now surrounded by worthless piles of buffalo hides. He offers the novel's bleakest diagnosis. "You're no better than the things you kill," he informs Andrews, then goes on to tell him why "young people . . . always think there's something to find out," when really: "There's nothing. . . . You get born, and you nurse on lies, and you get weaned on lies, and you learn fancier lies in school. You live all your life on lies, and then maybe when you're ready to die, it comes to you—there's nothing, nothing but yourself and what you could have done. Only you ain't done it, because the lies told you there was something else."

Rather than leaving us with this piece of late Mark Twain darkness, however, Williams ends the novel by following Andrews back to Butchers Crossing for a week of thoughtless beauty and pleasure with the one substantial female character, Francine; together, they carve out a space apart from the world.

Butcher's Crossing also follows him when he breaks trust with her and sneaks away, leaving the money she had pointedly refused to accept from him; money that reduces their week together to another salable commodity. That moment helps readers to link the pointless slaughter of unsalable buffaloes to the spooky absence of Native Americans from this whitened West. The pattern can, and is meant to, spiral outward, encompassing also the destructive zeal of Cold War America, reaching out eagerly, with Emersonian zeal, to the east, west, north, and south. In 1960 Louis L'Amour ruled the western novel, and Hollywood featured leather-skinned John Wayne's machismo and the liberal piety of Gary Cooper's *High Noon*. Is it surprising there was so little space for Williams's pessimism?

Butcher's Crossing ends with the reader certain, dead certain, that the destruction of the past cannot be undone. Yet there's a hint of hope: the novel takes seriously both the cost *and* the appeal of what it calls "vitality." When Andrews feels it moving through him during a river crossing late in the book, that is both promise and threat.

> As the animal stepped slowly forward, Andrews felt for brief instants the sickening sensation of weightlessness as he and the horse were buoyed and pushed aside by the swift current. The roaring was intense and hollow in his ears; he looked down from the point of land that dipped and swayed in his sight, and saw the water. It was a deep but transparent greenish brown, and it flowed past him in thick ropes and sheeted wedges, in shapes that changed with an incredible complexity before his gaze.

Five minutes later the river sends a log crashing into Andrews's partner Schneider—a log that kills horse and rider both, then casually tips their winter's worth of buffalo hides into the flood. But those "thick ropes and sheeted wedges" are still there, still haunting. They even hover below the surface in the novel's final line: "he rode forward without hurry, and felt behind him the sun slowly rise and harden the air." Go west, not-quite-so-young man.

There is no reason we should congratulate ourselves for being among the living: "vitality" is not a virtue, just a fact of life. Still, we make sense of Nature by being buoyed and pushed aside by it. Thoreau craves "Contact! Contact!" with Nature in its unapproachable inhumanity. Williams does not aim to show us Nature as it is when we are not around. Instead, he details what it feels like when it tugs at us, makes us respond to its lineaments and its power.

Chapter Thirty-Eight

JOURNEY IN SEARCH OF THE WAY

SATOMI MYŌDŌ

THEO DAVIS

AS SPIRITUAL autobiographies go, *Journey in Search of the Way* is a bit of a romp. Written in 1956, Satomi Myōdō's account of the fits and starts of her Buddhist practice weaves her awakening together with her adventures as a single mother, student, actress, and *miko* (shamaness). Early in life, she seduces a man in order to protest her high school's ideology of "Good Wives and Wise Mothers"; later on, she insists on studying Buddhism, even as her family chides, "At your age? . . . Grandmother! What's the matter with you?" Every story she relates conveys her sense that enlightenment is a normal aspiration for even the most unlikely of us.

Translated by Sallie B. King, who also contributed an extensive afterword putting the book in historical context, *Journey* has stayed with me for the unselfconscious cheer with which Myōdō recounts her misery. For instance, early on, Myōdō describes giving up her work as an actress to live with

Ryō-chan, a "waiflike" gang member she hopes to reform. Like most romantic rescue missions, this one quickly turns sour:

> I . . . quickly became aware of my own ugliness. Anger, jealousy, and all the other vices that seemed to have lain dormant now began to turn up constantly. I wanted to tell Ryō-chan off and drive him away. I ground my teeth and struggled to control these feelings, but in nine out of ten cases I was defeated. Even when I unexpectedly found myself succeeding in this struggle, my success proved temporary, and I soon reverted to nastiness. . . . . For me to try to rescue Ryō-chan was a complete impossibility and pure conceit. Carried away with emotion, I had completely overestimated myself. I did not stop and think. Unconsciously, I had decided that I was a correct and pure person. How shameful!

Myōdō is scrupulous in chronicling the "anger, jealousy, and . . . other vices" that "turn up constantly" and how her attempts to be decent lapse back into "nastiness." Still, there is something briskly untortured about the account; even the exclamation "how shameful!" seems to come with a smile.

Myōdō writes at one point, "Finally, winter passed. I began to hate myself." Yet it never seems that the narrating Myōdō hates her past self. I take the high-spirited clarity of Myōdō's accounts of her own failings as a form of insight into the first of the Four Noble Truths taught by the Buddha: there is suffering. It exists, and it is there to be seen and understood.

Myōdō's brief experiment with Christianity illuminates her approach; after hearing a sermon on how "bad wood is cut down and thrown in the fire of Gehenna," she decides that "I am that bad wood, no doubt." Yet she concludes, "I could not become a Christian," because she is not, in fact, interested in "the Kingdom of Heaven." Her aim is not to extirpate sin and save herself but to comprehend suffering: as she explains it, "I wanted to know why I was such bad wood."

Although many people turn to meditation and mindfulness practices in search of stress relief, the Buddhist teacher Jesse Maceo Vega-Frey warns against the notion that comfort will be the fruit of such efforts. At least, they won't offer the comfort of greater ease with the status quo: Vega-Frey calls that "the false promise of mindfulness."[1]

The idea that meditative practices can lead *away* from comfort permeates *Journey in Search of the Way*. We see Myōdō falling into a "delirium" in which she dreams of "a huge, round blood-red flower" in "a lacquer-black darkness"; "just then my whole body was seized by a violent and uncontrollable trembling." As a *miko*, intense concentration allows her to empty her mind and channel other consciousnesses, but that concentration is almost violent: "My mind was strained to the point of pain by the sheer not-self." After her first enlightenment, she finds herself, near the close of World War II, seeing both dead bodies and those "half dead and half alive" heaped in a train station. She is "desolate" as her "wonderful experience sank into the deep shadows of [her] subconscious." So much for relaxation.

Since *Journey* is unequivocally the story of an enlightened person, it raises the question of exactly what an enlightened person is like. At one point, Myōdō observes, "The more I practiced *zazen*, the less things turned out the way I expected." That observation can be connected to a later one: "Now that I have awakened from the dream and can see clearly, I know that the saying 'You don't have the same experience twice' is really true." The ability to see each moment of arising experience as new is a central insight in Buddhism. In Pali, the language in which the Buddha's teachings were first written down, this impermanence is called *anicca*. This is why the more Myōdō practices, the more unexpected life becomes: she is experiencing *anicca* more and more intimately.

It is not only happiness in understanding suffering and the resulting relief from the weight of confused expectation that I sense in the breeziness of this book's tone. There is also delight in the freshness of seeing. At one point, Myōdō describes her response to a lecture on the koan "Kashō and the Flagpole":

The tatami mats of the main hall at Raikōji were worn at the edges and tattered. When I saw that, I found myself thinking, "When I worked as a *miko*, business really thrived; I could have easily had these mats fixed. Maybe I should become a *miko* again! Even that isn't altogether useless in the work of liberating the dead who have lost their way."

Just then—"Aha!"—I caught myself. "You fool! That's the flagpole! Yes—when the merest glance casts a reflection in your mind, that's the flagpole! Knock over that flagpole in your mind! One after another, knock them down!"

She has suddenly grasped that woolgathering about past and future obscures the immediacy that a "merest glance" can have, even if it's just of an old mat. "Now I had discovered a principle to guide my practice." As the excitement in the passage intimates, just knowing can contain a delight that does not depend on the quality of the object known but rather on the clarity of awareness. Seeing that, our whole way of relating to the world can be shaken.

As Myōdō tells it, frustration and misery are not the final word but are part of a wholly ordinary, if dramatic, confusion, from which one may emerge. Her voice is quite a tonic for these times.

NOTE

1. Jesse Maceo Vega-Frey, "The PBG and the False Promise of Mindfulness," Buddhist Peace Fellowship (June 2014), http://www .buddhistpeacefellowship.org/the-pbg-and-the-false-promise-of -mindfulness/.

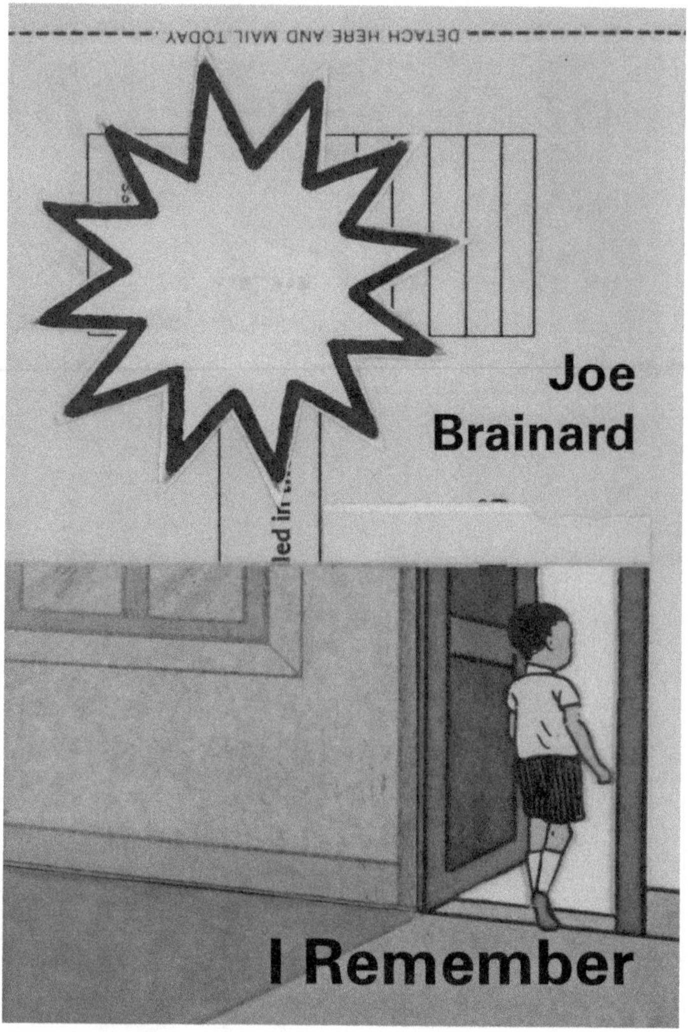

DETACH HERE AND MAIL TODAY
Joe Brainard
I Remember

Chapter Thirty-Nine

I REMEMBER

JOE BRAINARD

ANDREW H. MILLER

JOHN ASHBERY said he was nice—"nice as a person and nice as an artist." I think it's fair to say that we don't have a rich critical vocabulary for nice artists. (And how many are there?) Yet everyone agrees that Joe Brainard was one. There seems to have been a magnetism in his niceness, so many people came to love him.

Brainard was a collagist, painter, illustrator, and poet. He was part of the New York School, a group of friends who came of age in the fifties and sixties, poets and artists eager to capture the everyday, without betraying it into high seriousness. In his prose, Brainard was a collector of stray moments, with a knack for conveying what Virginia Woolf called "the suggestiveness of reality": "I was saying to Bob the other night how easy it would be to live in Bolinas if you were madly in love (a few minutes of silence while we could tell that we were both thinking the same thing) as one of us said 'But, of course that could be said about just about *any* place.' Nice when that happens."

Much of what is most winning about Brainard's writing is in these two sentences: his innocence, his inwardness, his easy-going attention, his ungainly grace, his skew humor, his power of evocation, his conversational voice and conversational silence. Because he was undefended and open to being seen, he was open to seeing; moments stuck to him like burrs stick to your clothes as you cross a field. He used parentheses generously to include the intricacies of his thought and seems never to have used a semicolon (too formal): "Dinner tonight at 'The Gibson House.' (Steak). And too much wine. (Depending on how you look at it.)" He loved things, but he loved people more. His sentences always seem ready to turn from the third person to the second. And sometimes they do: "Poem by Anne about my show today. So extravagant! (And I love you for it.)"

When I first read these three passages in Brainard's *Collected Writings*, I assumed they were private writings, only to discover that they had been published in his book *Bolinas Journal*. After that, I repeatedly found myself flipping to the endnotes to find out whether I was reading a public, published work or a private, unpublished one, but there's little difference, really.

Although his visual art belongs to the permanent collections of various museums—MoMA, the Met, the Whitney—he's now best known for his book *I Remember*, a loose-limbed volume of memories. Brainard had the idea for the book one day while sunbathing in Vermont. "I wrote a bit on a new thing

I am writing called 'I Remember,'" he told his friend, the poet James Schuyler. "It's just a collection of things I remember." Brainard would write each day and show his work to Schuyler at night. "He would tell me how terrific it was, which was all I needed for the next day," he later remarked in an interview (with Tim Dlugos, included in *The Collected Writings*). Reading the book, you can feel that it was written within friendship's deep shelter, where the most important questions have already been answered and everything is of interest. He doesn't expect his readers to be mean, and so we aren't.

Granted the license of friendship, Brainard is free to be oblique and partial. Most of his memories have one brief act:

> I remember how disappointing going to bed with one of the most beautiful boys I have ever seen was. . . .
> I remember catching myself with an expression on my face that doesn't relate to what's going on anymore.

Others seem to have two or more:

> I remember wanting to sleep out in the backyard and being kidded about how I wouldn't last the night and sleeping outside and not lasting the night. . . .
> I remember, when a fart invades a room, trying to look like I didn't do it, even if, indeed, I *didn't*. . . .
> I remember, at parties, after you've said all you can think of to say to a person—but there you both stand. . . .
> I remember, after a lot of necking, how untheatrical the act of getting undressed can sometimes be.

But all of them meditate on the ways language accommodates the varieties of remembered experience. Some live in the past: "I remember red rubber coin purses that opened like a pair of lips, with a squeeze." Others measure the distance between past and present: "I remember early sexual experiences and rubbery knees. I'm sure sex is better now but I *do* miss rubbery knees." Others reflect on time's strange passage: "I remember getting a car door slammed on my finger once, and how long it took for the pain to come." Still others float uncertainly between past and present: "I remember over-tipping. And I still do." Collected together, they suspend time, leaving his memories gently vibrating, still.

I Remember is "about everybody else as much as it is about me," he wrote his friend Anne Waldman. "And that pleases me. I mean, I feel like I am everybody. And it's a nice feeling. It won't last. But I am enjoying it while I can." Part of the pleasure in reading the book, of course, comes in finding your own memories shared by someone else (nice when that happens). Another part of the pleasure comes from listening for the harmonics of the thing, the way that the memories work together and apart, never giving you everything but always giving you something.

I remember finding things in the drawer I wasn't supposed to see, smothered in nylons.

I remember the olive green velvet lining of my mother's olive green "leather" jewelry box, with fold-out trays. When alone in the house, I loved going through it, examining each piece carefully, trying to pick out my favorites. And sometimes, trying on something, but mostly I just liked to look.

I remember learning very early in life the art of putting back everything exactly the way it was.

Perhaps, you think, his work as a collagist began here. Perhaps growing up, for him, meant learning to put things where they don't belong. But you can't know. And the next paragraph brings a new topic. The result is a book of immense generosity, in which anything could be included:

I remember daydreams of going with an absolutely knock-out girl, and impressing all my friends no end.

I remember wondering how one would go about putting on a rubber gracefully, in the given situation. . . .

I remember a little boy who said it was more fun to pee together than alone, and so we did, and so it was. . . .

I remember rocks you pick up outside that, once inside, you wonder why.

A large collection of small things, *I Remember* is neither large nor small; it's lengthless. Brainard published it and then wrote *I Remember More*, followed by *More I Remember More*, and then other people continued to develop the form in their own way. Kenneth Koch used it to teach kids to write poetry. Georges Perec's autobiographical *Je me souviens* (*I Remember*) is dedicated to Brainard; it has blank pages at the end for readers to add their own memories.

Though *I Remember* contains much, its achievement, or one of them, lies in its attitude toward all it can't contain. In his elegy for Brainard, who died of AIDS-related pneumonia in 1994, the poet Frank Bidart writes of his friend's *"purity and / sweetness self-gathered"*:

> you had somehow erased within you not only
> meanness, but anger, the desire to punish
> the universe for everything
> *not* achieved, *not* tasted, seen again, touched—;

In the eighties, when he was in his forties, Brainard gradually stopped publishing his writing and making art. Friends and critics have often wondered why. But the extraordinary thing is how little art there was to begin with—how close his art was to living. Brainard seems to me most like his friend Schuyler. Both are diarists, taking apparently unremarkable details of daily life and polishing them just a bit. It is as if life has taken the smallest step into art. We're used to the kind of trompe l'oeil in which a painting looks lifelike: birds fly down to peck at the grapes. But Brainard reminds us that trompe l'oeil can go the other direction, too: I see two women walking down the street who seem to dance; across the way, a boy stands contrapposto.

Mean, awkward, fond, gentle, equable, comforting: this seems the right, modest register to use in talking about nice art. What's remarkable, then, is how, when you're in the right mood, Brainard's writing can seem to give you all you need. His *Collected Writings* closes with a paragraph found in his papers after he died. Brainard titled it "January 13th," and it ends this way: "Outside my window snow is falling down, against a translucent sky of deep lavender, with a touch of orange, zig-zagged along the bottom into a silhouette of black buildings. (The icebox clicks off, and shudders.) And it's as simple as this, what I want to tell you about: if perhaps not much, everything. Painting the moment for you tonight."

Chapter Forty

TRANSFORMATRIX

PATIENCE AGBABI

STEPHANIE BURT

FEW POETS seem to have more fun than Patience Agbabi. Few poets succeed so well—or started so early—in merging the sonic patterns of Afro-diasporic performance, of hip-hop gone syncretically international, with European page-based formal tradition. For more than two decades, Agbabi has woven the in-your-face bravura aesthetic she gets from the former into the most challenging, puzzle-like parts of the latter. But the importance of *Transformatrix* and of Agbabi's work doesn't just lie in the way she shows her sources to go together; it's also in the way that she takes herself and her experience as the norm. European verse tradition must bend to fit her, to accommodate her British Nigerian experience and varieties of spoken language, never the other way round.

In Britain, she's known both as a writer of books and as a spoken-word poet, with dynamic delivery and a recognizable buzz cut. Her poetry shows up on national high school exams;

she's read at the National Gallery in London and on the BBC. Since 1995 she's published four books, the most recent a concise, attractive retelling of Chaucer's *Canterbury Tales*, with stanzaic and metrical variety to match Chaucer's own. That book, *Telling Tales*, gave her a following among medievalists. It is the only one she's gained, so far, in North America.

That should change. Agbabi is one of the handful of poets—and often seen as one of the first—who can not only use but also adapt and render distinctive both the rhythms and references of hip-hop and the strictness of page-based European forms. She's no more a radio-ready rapper than she is Algernon Charles Swinburne, but she has virtues common to both: the energy, the in-jokes, the personality, the array of characters, the social protest, and sometimes (as with Swinburne) the kinky sex.

You can find all these virtues in her second book, *Transformatrix*, published in Scotland in 2000. The collection begins with a page-long boast: "If you join two words you get multiplication. / My school of mathematics / equals verbal acrobatics / so let's make conversation." Next up are stanzaic poems about invented characters, such as the Afrofuturist verse "UFO Woman (Pronounced Oofoe)," a Nigerian-accented woman from space now living in London: "Meandering the streets paved with / hopscotch and butterscotch, kids with crystal / cut ice-cream cones and tin-can eyes ask 'Why / don't U F O back to your own planet?'"

It's a rude pun and an old problem for immigrants facing "streets paved with NF (no fun) graffiti. / *Nefertiti go home* from the old days." (The NF is the racist British group the

National Front.) Agbabi's Afrofuturist becomes a kind of punning Afro-pessimist, deciding to seek a better fate off-planet: "Why wait for First World *Homo sapiens* / to cease their retroactive spacism?" Instead, she readies herself "for lift-off / in my fibre-optic firefly Levis."

The comedy in Agbabi's "Wife of Bafa" is less verbal than situational. "Mrs Alice Ebi Bafa," like Chaucer's wife of Bath, has had five husbands (one at a time) and taught the last one to behave: Mrs. Bafa threw her husband's porno mags in the grate; he hit her; then she "beat him till he screamed for his ancestors. / Now we get on like house on fire." "Some say I have blood on my hands," she shrugs, "'cause I like to paint my nails red / but others call me femme fatale." Like the Chaucerian originals, Alice has an ulterior motive: "Would you like to buy some cloth?"

Transformatrix is not a perfect book, and what might be Agbabi's best individual poems aren't even in it. The volume does not contain, for example, her polyrhythmic rewrite of Chaucer's "General Prologue," where each line hurtles towards a funky spondee:

> though my mind's overtaxed, April fires me
> how she pierces my heart to the fond root
> till I bleed cherry blossom en route,
> to our bliss trip; there's days she goes off me,
> April loves me not; April loves me . . .

Nor does it hold her later poem "Josephine Baker Finds Herself," whose tour de force of sexy mirror writing (the poem reads the same, line by line, forwards and in reverse) has to be read or heard whole to be understood. At its center: "I worship / the way she looks. / The way she looks / me up and down. I worship / twenties chic." Baker becomes Agbabi's precedent for a queer black artist who takes over a white cultural hub and makes herself the sometimes gleeful, sometimes melancholy center of attention.

A poet of personae, Agbabi is also a poet of forms and strict constraints, not only the mirrored line order of "Josephine Baker Explains Herself" but also the six rotating end words of her sestinas. *Transformatrix* includes seven sestinas, all with the same line endings: child, boy, end, dark, time, girl. One portrays a time traveler, another a woman's memories of her tattoos:

> I rolled up my sleeve like a child
> giving blood for the first time.
> *Tracy Loves Darren.* It was girl
> power, 1979. He was my aerosol boy
> and the swelling inscription, my lifebuoy.
> We lasted a month.

There's also Leila, the eternal principle of the feminine, whose name in Hebrew and Arabic means "night":

> If she were a time
> she'd be midnight, big hand on little, girl
> surrendering to womanhood, the fierce end
> of needles pointing blood. She's yesterday's child

ticking red ellipses, leaving a trail for boys
to find her. And she controls the dark
as if she were princess of the dark.

Here are women and girls reclaiming the stereotypes that have
made us mysterious and kept us down. Here, too, are women
and girls reclaiming blackness as a source of power right alongside (rather than displacing) European traditions. In the final
poem, the title poem, Agbabi inflicts her pleasurable discipline
(she's a transformer and also a dominatrix) upon a client called
the English language: "without me / she's . . . rigid as a full
stop."

Agbabi's characters—her Josephine Baker, her fast-living
teens from council houses, her night goddess—set their own
terms for their own life and speech. Agbabi does too: such terms
feel both contemporary and virtuosic. Reading her work can feel
like meeting somebody way cooler than you will ever be but
also like watching somebody who has mastered something
intrinsically hard by following rules specific to her art, like a
great DJ, trumpeter, or gymnast. And when those rules operate, whiteness and white language—even to a white reader—no
longer seem normal, standard, or unmarked; in *Transformatrix*
Black British language and Black British sounds are the new
standard, the ground from which so much else springs.

CONTRIBUTORS

Steven Biel is executive director of the Mahindra Humanities Center and senior lecturer on history and literature at Harvard University. He is the author of *American Gothic: A Life of America's Most Famous Painting*; *Down with the Old Canoe: A Cultural History of the Titanic Disaster*; and *Independent Intellectuals in the United States, 1910–1945* and the editor of *American Disasters* and *Titanica: The Disaster of the Century in Poetry, Song, and Prose*.

Jonathan Bolton is professor of Slavic languages and literatures at Harvard University, where he teaches Czech and Central European history and culture. His book *Worlds of Dissent: Charter 77, the Plastic People of the Universe, and Czech Culture Under Communism* offers a new approach to the dissident movements in East Central Europe in the 1970s and 1980s. He has also edited and translated *In the Puppet Gardens: Selected Poems, 1963–2005*, by the Czech poet Ivan Wernisch.

Kevin Brazil is the author of *Art, History, and Postwar Fiction*, and his essays and criticism have appeared in the *Times Literary Supplement*, the *London Review of Books*, the *White Review*, *Art Review*, and *art-agenda*. He teaches English at the University of Southampton.

CONTRIBUTORS

Adrienne Brown is associate professor of English at the University of Chicago. She is the coeditor with Valerie Smith of *Race and Real Estate* and author of *The Black Skyscraper: Architecture and the Perception of Race*.

Stephanie Burt is professor of English at Harvard. Her books of poetry and literary criticism include, most recently, *After Callimachus* and *Don't Read Poetry: A Book About How to Read Poems*. She lives in Belmont, Mass. with one spouse, two kids, two cats, and an uncanny quantity of *X-Men* comics.

Margaret Cohen teaches in the Department of English at Stanford University, where she holds the Andrew. B Hammond Chair. Her books include the award-winning *The Novel and the Sea* (2009) and *The Sentimental Education of the Novel* (1998), as well as *Profane Illumination* (1993). She is currently editing *A Cultural History of the Sea* (6 volumes, forthcoming) and completing a book on the history of underwater film.

Caleb Crain is the author of the novels *Necessary Errors* and *Overthrow* and of the critical work *American Sympathy*.

Seeta Chaganti is professor of English at the University of California, Davis. Her book *Strange Footing* (2018) received the MLA Scaglione Prize in Comparative Literary Studies. Her scholarship explores medieval poetry's relationship to culture, from dance to devotional artifacts. She also writes for general audiences on the opportunities medieval studies can provide to resist white supremacy and promote racial justice.

Pardis Dabashi is assistant professor of English at the University of Nevada, Reno, where she specializes in twentieth-century American literature and film studies. Her work has appeared or is forthcoming in *PMLA, Modernism/modernity, Modern Fiction Studies, Arizona Quarterly, Public Books, Politics/Letters*, and elsewhere. She is coeditor of *The New Faulkner Studies* (forthcoming 2021) and is completing her book manuscript *Moving Images: Film and the Affective World of the Modernist Novel*.

Lorraine Daston is director emerita at the Max Planck Institute for the History of Science in Berlin and regular visiting professor in the Committee on Social Thought at the University of Chicago. She has published widely on topics in the history of early modern and modern science, including probability

CONTRIBUTORS

and statistics, wonders, objectivity, observation, and scientific archives. She is the recipient of both the Pfizer Prize and the Sarton Medal of the History of Science Society and of the Dan David Prize. Her most recent book is *Against Nature* (2019).

Theo Davis is professor of English at Northeastern University. She is the author of *Ornamental Aesthetics: The Poetry of Attending in Thoreau, Dickinson, and Whitman* (2016) and *Formalism, Experience, and the Making of American Literature in the Nineteenth Century* (2007). Her current project, *Somatic Awareness: An Essay on Embodiment* has been supported by a fellowship from the Guggenheim Foundation.

Maud Ellmann is the Randy L. And Melvin R. Berlin Professor of the Development of the Novel in English at the University of Chicago. She has written widely on modernism, Irish studies, and literary theory, with a focus on psychoanalysis. Her most recent book is *The Nets of Modernism: James, Woolf, Joyce, and Freud* (2010).

Merve Emre is associate professor of English at the University of Oxford.

Elizabeth Ferry is professor of anthropology at Brandeis University, with interests in value, materiality, mining, and finance and with fieldwork emphases in Mexico, Colombia, and the United States. She is the author of *Not Ours Alone: Patrimony, Value, and Collectivity in Contemporary Mexico* (2005); *Minerals, Collecting, and Value Across the U.S.-Mexico Border* (2013); and with Stephen Ferry, *La Batea*, a book of photographs and writings about small-scale gold mining in Colombia (2017).

Penny Fielding is Grierson Professor of English at the University of Edinburgh. Her most recent book is *The 1880s* (2019).

Ben Fountain's work has received the PEN/Hemingway Award, the National Book Critics Circle Award for Fiction, the Los Angeles Times Book Prize for Fiction, and a Whiting Writers Award and has been a finalist for the National Book Award, among other honors. He lives in Dallas.

Elizabeth Graver's fourth novel, *The End of the Point*, was long-listed for the 2013 National Book Award in Fiction. Her other novels are *Awake,*

The Honey Thief, and *Unravelling.* Her story collection, *Have You Seen Me?,* won the 1991 Drue Heinz Literature Prize. Her work has appeared in *Best American Short Stories; Prize Stories: The O. Henry Awards; The Pushcart Prize Anthology;* and *Best American Essays.* She teaches at Boston College.

Isabel Hofmeyr is professor of African literature at the University of the Witwatersrand, Johannesburg, and Global Distinguished Professor at NYU. She lives in Johannesburg where she heads up the Mellon-funded project "Oceanic Humanities for the Global South." A new book entitled *Hydrocolonialism: Coast, Custom House, and Dockside Reading* is forthcoming.

Emily Hyde is an assistant professor of English at Rowan University. Her articles and reviews on comparative modernisms, postcolonial literature, and contemporary literature and photography appear in *PMLA, Literature Compass, Post45: Peer Reviewed, Comparative Literature Studies, Public Books,* and *Post45: Contemporaries.* She is at work on *A Way of Seeing: Postcolonial Modernism and the Visual Book,* a project examining the global forms of mid-twentieth-century literature through the vexed status of the visual.

Lauren Kaminsky is the director of studies and an associate senior lecturer in the Committee on Degrees in History and Literature at Harvard University. A historian of gender, sexuality, and the Soviet Union, she is also a faculty associate at the Davis Center for Russian and Eurasian Studies.

Ivan Kreilkamp is professor of English in the Department of English at Indiana University, Bloomington, where he is also coeditor of *Victorian Studies.* His most recent books are *"A Visit From the Goon Squad" Reread* (Columbia, 2020) and *Minor Creatures: Persons, Animals, and the Victorian Novel* (2018).

Yoon Sun Lee teaches at Wellesley College. She is the author of *Nationalism and Irony: Burke, Scott, Carlyle* and *Modern Minority: Asian American Literature and Everyday Life,* as well as articles published in *Novel: A Forum on Fiction, Representations, The Cambridge Companion to Narrative Theory, The Cambridge Companion to the Postcolonial Novel, MLQ, ELH,* and other journals. Her current book project examines plot and objectivity in the realist novel.

Ursula K. Le Guin was born in 1929 in Berkeley and died in 2018 in Portland, Oregon. As of 2017, she had published twenty-three novels, twelve collections of stories, five books of essays, thirteen books for children, nine volumes of poetry, and four of translation. Among her awards are the Hugo, Nebula, National Book, and PEN-Malamud, and she has been honored as a Library of Congress Living Legend and with the National Book Foundation Medal.

Kathryn Lofton is professor of religious studies, American studies, history, and divinity at Yale University. A historian of religions, she is the author of two books, *Oprah: The Gospel of an Icon* (2011) and *Consuming Religion* (2017), and one coedited collection (with Laurie Maffly-Kipp), *Women's Work: An Anthology of African-American Women's Historical Writings* (2010).

Sharon Marcus is a founding editor of *Public Books* and Orlando Harriman Professor of English and Comparative Literature at Columbia University. The recipient of fellowships from the Guggenheim Foundation, the Radcliffe Institute for Advanced Study, and the American Council of Learned Societies, she is the author of *Apartment Stories* (1999), *Between Women* (2007), and *The Drama of Celebrity* (2019).

Kate Marshall is associate professor of English at the University of Notre Dame, where she is also faculty in the history and philosophy of science. She is the author of *Corridor: Media Architectures in American Fiction* (2013), and her second book, *A Poetics of the Outside*, is under contract. She edits the Post45 book series for Stanford University Press.

Sean McCann is professor of English at Wesleyan University. He is the author of *A Pinnacle of Feeling: American Literature and Presidential Government* (2008) and *Gumshoe America: Hard-Boiled Crime Fiction and the Rise and Fall of New Deal Liberalism* (2000).

Stephen McCauley is the author of nine novels, including *The Object of My Affection* and *My Ex-Life*. He currently serves as codirector of creative writing at Brandeis University.

Andrew H. Miller is the author, most recently, of *On Not Being Someone Else: Tales of Our Unled Lives*, as well as essays in *Brick, Michigan Quarterly Review, Representations, PMLA*, and elsewhere. He is professor of English at Johns Hopkins University.

CONTRIBUTORS

Toril Moi teaches at Duke University. Among her books are *Simone de Beauvoir: The Making of an Intellectual Woman* (1994); *Henrik Ibsen and the Birth of Modernism* (2006); and *Revolution of the Ordinary: Literary Studies After Wittgenstein, Austin, and Cavell* (2017). She also works extensively on Norwegian and contemporary literature and writes regularly for the Norwegian weekly *Morgenbladet* and less regularly for *The Point* magazine.

Upamanyu Pablo Mukherjee researches on Victorian and contemporary imperialism and colonialism, environmental/ecological criticism, and world literary studies. He is the author of five monographs, three edited collections, and a wide range of scholarly essays, including *Final Frontiers: Science Fiction and Techno-Science in Non-Aligned India* (2020); *Combined and Uneven Development: Towards a New Theory of World-Literature* (with WReC, 2015); *Natural Disasters and Victorian Imperial Culture* (2013); *Postcolonial Environments: Nature, Culture, and the Contemporary Indian Novel in English* (2010); and *Crime and Empire* (2003). He is currently working with his WReC colleagues on a volume called *Keywords in World-Literature* and editing a special issue of *Revue Etudes Anglaises* on "Energy Humanities."

John Plotz is Barbara Mandel Professor of the Humanities at Brandeis University; his books include *Time and the Tapestry: A William Morris Adventure* and *Semi-Detached: The Aesthetics of Virtual Experience Since Dickens*. He edits the B-Sides feature in *Public Books* and hosts the podcast *Recall This Book*.

Leah Price's books include *What We Talk About When We Talk About Books* (2019); *How to Do Things with Books in Victorian Britain* (2012); and *The Anthology and the Rise of the Novel* (2000). She writes for the *New York Times Book Review*, *London Review of Books*, *Times Literary Supplement*, and *New York Review of Books*. She teaches at Rutgers.

Carlo Rotella's most recent book is *The World Is Always Coming to an End: Pulling Together and Apart in a Chicago Neighborhood*. A professor of English at Boston College, he contributes regularly to the New York Times Magazine, and his work has also appeared in the *New Yorker*, *Harper's*, and *The Best American Essays*.

Paul Saint-Amour is Walter H. and Leonore C. Annenberg Professor in the Humanities and chairs the Department of English at the University of Pennsylvania. He is the author of *The Copywrights: Intellectual Property and* *the Literary Imagination* and *Tense Future: Modernism, Total War, Encyclopedic Form*. Saint-Amour edited *Modernism and Copyright* and coedits, with Jessica Berman, the Modernist Latitudes series at Columbia University Press.

Salvatore Scibona's most recent novel, *The Volunteer*, has been published or is forthcoming in seven languages. His first novel, *The End*, was a finalist for the National Book Award and the winner of the Young Lions Fiction Award. He has won a Guggenheim Fellowship, a Pushcart Prize, an O. Henry Award, and a Whiting Award and has been named one of the *New Yorker's* "20 under 40" fiction writers. He directs the Cullman Center for Scholars and Writers at the New York Public Library.

Namwali Serpell is a Zambian writer who teaches at UC Berkeley. She's the author of *Seven Modes of Uncertainty* (2014) and a novel, *The Old Drift* (Hogarth, 2019), which won the 2020 Anisfield-Wolf Book prize and the *L.A. Times'* Art Seidenbaum Award for First Fiction. She has received a 2020 Windham-Campbell Prize for fiction, the 2015 Caine Prize for African Writing, and a 2011 Rona Jaffe Foundation Writers' Award.

Vanessa Smith is professor of English Literature at the University of Sydney. She has published widely on the literature of Oceanic/European contact and on object-relations psychoanalysis and literary form. She has written at greater length on Milner's *A Life of One's Own* in "Transferred Debts: Marion Milner's A Life of One's Own and the limits of analysis," *Feminist Modernist Studies* 1, no. (1–2): 96–111.

Ramie Targoff is professor of English at Brandeis University. She is the author of *Common Prayer*; *John Donne, Body and Soul*; *Posthumous Love*; and *Renaissance Woman: The Life of Vittoria Colonna*. Her translation of Colonna's 1538 *Rime* is forthcoming in 2021. She is currently working on a joint biography of four women writers from the English Renaissance, *Shakespeare's Sisters*.

Rebecca Zorach teaches and writes on early modern European art, the Black Arts Movement, and contemporary activist art. Her books include *Blood, Milk, Ink, Gold: Abundance and Excess in the French Renaissance* (2005); *The Passionate Triangle* (2011); the exhibition catalogue *The Time Is Now! Art Worlds of Chicago's South Side, 1960–1980* (2018); and *Art for People's Sake: Artists and Community in Black Chicago, 1965–1975* (2019).